God's Prophetic Voices to America

Dr. David R. Reagan

LAMB
& LION
MINISTRIES

www.lamblion.com

Dedicated to

Darryl Nunnelley

A man with a generous heart,
a zeal for Jesus,
and a passion for His return.

———————————

First edition, 2017

Copyright © 2017 by Lamb & Lion Ministries

ISBN: 978-0-945593-29-4

Library of Congress Control Number: 2017908216

Lamb & Lion Ministries
P.O. Box 919
McKinney, Texas 75070
lamblion@lamblion.com
www.lamblion.com

Cover design by William Looney.

All scripture quotations, unless otherwise noted, are from the New
American Standard Version, © 1995 by the Lockman Foundation.

Scripture references labeled "LBP" are from *The Living Bible
Paraphrased* © 1971 by Tyndale House Publishers.

Printed in the United States of America.

Contents

Part 3: A Summary

Deuteronomy 8:11, 17-20

11) "Beware that you do not forget the LORD your God by not keeping His commandments and His ordinances and His statutes . . .

17) "Otherwise, you may say in your heart, 'My power and the strength of my hand made me this wealth.'

18) "But you shall remember the LORD your God, for it is He who is giving you power to make wealth, that He may confirm His covenant which He swore to your fathers, as it is this day.

19) "It shall come about if you ever forget the LORD your God and go after other gods and serve them and worship them, I testify against you today that you will surely perish.

20) "Like the nations that the LORD makes to perish before you, so you shall perish; because you would not listen to the voice of the LORD your God."

Books by Dr. David R. Reagan

The Christ in Prophecy Study Guide (McKinney, TX: Lamb & Lion Ministries, 1987). Second edition in 2001.

Trusting God: Learning to Walk by Faith (Lafayette, LA: Huntington House, 1987). Second edition in 1994.

Jesus is Coming Again! (Eugene, OR: Harvest House, 1992).

The Master Plan: Making Sense of the Controversies Surrounding Bible Prophecy Today (Eugene, OR: Harvest House, 1993).

Living for Christ in the End Times (Green Forest, AR: New Leaf Press, 2000). Second edition in 2015.

Wrath and Glory: Unveiling the Majestic Book of Revelation (Green Forest, AR: New Leaf Press, 2001). Second edition in 2016.

America the Beautiful? The United States in Bible Prophecy (McKinney, TX: Lamb & Lion Ministries, 2003). Second edition in 2006. Third edition in 2009.

God's Plan for the Ages: The Blueprint of Bible Prophecy (McKinney, TX: Lamb & Lion Ministries, 2005).

Eternity: Heaven or Hell? (McKinney, TX: Lamb & Lion Ministries, 2010).

Jesus: The Lamb and The Lion (McKinney, TX: Lamb & Lion Ministries, 2011).

The Man of Lawlessness: The Antichrist in the Tribulation (McKinney, TX: Lamb & Lion Ministries, 2012).

A Prophetic Manifesto (McKinney, TX: Lamb & Lion Ministries, 2012).

Living on Borrowed Time: the Imminent Return of Jesus (McKinney, TX: Lamb & Lion Ministries, 2013).

The Jewish People: Rejected or Beloved? (McKinney, TX: Lamb & Lion Ministries, 2014).

Israel in Bible Prophecy: Past, Present & Future (McKinney, TX: Lamb & Lion Ministries, 2017).

Preface

God never pours out His wrath without warning because He does not wish that any should perish but that all should come to repentance (2 Peter 3:9).

God warns in two ways: through prophetic voices and remedial judgments.

God has been speaking to America through prophetic voices for the past 50 years, earnestly calling this nation to repentance. We have turned a deaf ear to His pleas. And He has responded with remedial judgments.

Today, we are a nation in open rebellion against the very One who has been the source of all our blessings. In short, we are literally crying out for God to deliver us from judgment to destruction.

Fortunately, we are dealing with a God who is very patient. Consider these words from chapter 1 of the book of Nahum:

> 2) A jealous and avenging God is the LORD; The LORD is avenging and wrathful. The LORD takes vengeance on His adversaries, and He reserves wrath for His enemies.
>
> 3) The LORD is slow to anger and great in power, and the LORD will by no means leave the guilty unpunished . . .

Yes, God is very patient, but He will eventually deal with unrepented sin. There is a tipping point of no return at which time God delivers a nation from judgment to destruction.

Our nation is currently hurtling down the path of destruction with ever-increasing speed.

Is there any hope for America?

Before I specifically address that question, let's consider the seriousness of our nation's spiritual condition and the prophetic voices God has raised up.

Dr. David R. Reagan
Allen, TX
2017

Prologue

America's Spiritual Crisis

Beware that you do not forget the LORD your God by not keeping His commandments and His ordinances and His statutes which I am commanding you today; otherwise, when you have eaten and are satisfied, and have built good houses and lived in them . . . and your silver and gold multiply, and all that you have multiplies, then your heart will become proud and you will forget the LORD your God . . .

Deuteronomy 8:11-14

In order to understand the messages of the prophetic voices that God has raised up to speak to our nation, it is necessary to get a grasp of the enemy the voices are railing against. That enemy is what the world calls the philosophy of Humanism. In reality, it is the religion of Satan.

The core belief of Humanism is its conviction that Man is capable of solving his own problems apart from any supernatural intervention by God. Man is the focus, and Man is exalted. Man is considered to be capable of perfection through education and reliance on reason. Faith is condemned. Reason is worshiped.

God is considered to be an irrelevant myth that has been used by religions to enslave Mankind. Absolute Truth is rejected in favor of a system of ethics that is based solely on Man's needs and is thus situational in nature and subject to constant change.

The ultimate goal of life is the complete realization of human personality. Life beyond death is considered to be nonsense.

The First Humanist Manifesto

There have been many efforts over the past hundred years to define the tenets of Humanism. The first comprehensive effort occurred in 1933. It produced the First Humanist Manifesto.[1]

John Dewey
(Wikipedia)

This document basically declared that existing religions were out-of-date due "to man's larger understanding of the universe, his scientific achievements, and deeper appreciation of brotherhood."[2] The signers included nine Unitarian ministers and many university professors. The most notable signatory was John Dewey (1859-1952) of Columbia University, a liberal philosopher and educational reformer.

One interesting feature of this manifesto is that it referred to "Religious Humanism" throughout. This was a very accurate portrayal of what Humanism really is — namely, a secular religion. But this phraseology was abandoned in all subsequent Humanist documents in an attempt to present Humanism as a secular philosophy devoid of any religious pretensions.

The First Humanist Manifesto began with one of the cornerstone beliefs of the whole movement: "the universe as self-existing and not created."[3] The second principle was an affirmation of evolution, avowing that "man is a part of nature and that he has emerged as a result of a continuous process."[4] Other principles in the document denied the existence of absolute truths and rejected the supernatural.[5] Throughout there was an emphasis on the absolute necessity to rely on reason in order to be delivered from "sentimental and unreal hopes and wishful thinking."[6]

The manifesto ended with the proclamation that "man is at last becoming aware that he alone is responsible for the realization of the world of his dreams, that he has within himself the power for its achievement."[7]

The Second Humanist Manifesto

Forty years later, in 1973, the Second Humanist Manifesto was issued. In its preface, the authors made it clear that their number one target was Christianity:[8]

> As in 1933, Humanists still believe that traditional theism, especially faith in the prayer-hearing God, assumed to live and care for persons, to hear and understand their prayers, and to be able to do something about them, is an unproved and outmoded faith. Salvationism based on mere affirmation, still appears as harmful, diverting people with false hopes of heaven hereafter. Reasonable minds look to other means for survival.

This manifesto then began with the confident exclamation that "the next century [the 21st] can be and should be the Humanistic century."[9] It proceeded to affirm faith in the ability of Man to solve all his own problems:[10]

> Using technology wisely, we can control our environment, conquer poverty, markedly reduce disease, extend our life-span, significantly modify our behavior, alter the course of human evolution and cultural development, unlock vast new powers, and provide human-kind with unparalleled opportunity for achiev-

ing an abundant and meaningful life.

"False theologies of hope" and "messianic ideologies" were dismissed as being incapable of coping with "existing world realities [because] they separate rather than unite peoples."[11]

The attack on religion continued with the very first article of this manifesto, and its spared no words. A belief in the supernatural was declared to be "meaningless" and "irrelevant to the question of survival and fulfillment of the human race."[12] Their belief in Man was summed up in one short sentence: "As non-theists, we begin with humans, not God, nature not deity."[13] This section on religion concluded with this assertion:[14]

> . . . we can discover no divine purpose or providence for the human species. While there is much that we do not know, humans are responsible for what we are or will become. No deity will save us; we must save ourselves.

The second article of the 1973 manifesto was equally candid in its attack on the Christian concept of eternal life:[15]

> Promises of immortal salvation or fear of eternal damnation are both illusory and harmful. They distract humans from present concerns, from self-actualization, and from rectifying social injustices . . . There is no credible evidence that life survives the death of the body.

The sixth article of the 1973 manifesto was directed to a concern that was not expressed in the 1933 version, but which was implicit in it — namely, human sexuality. In a very blunt manner, the manifesto declared that orthodox religion has served to "unduly repress sexual conduct."[16]

Prologue: America's Spiritual Crisis   **13**

Articles six and seven launched an attack on the sanctity of life by calling for a "full range of civil liberties," including "abortion, euthanasia and the right to suicide."[17]

Venturing into the realm of world politics, the twelfth article denounced nationalism and called for "the building of a world community . . ."[18] In the closing paragraph of the manifesto, the advocacy of world government was mentioned again in the most idealistic terms: "What more daring goal for humankind than for each person to become, in ideas as well as practice, a citizen of a world community."[19]

Other Humanist Manifestos

A Third Humanist Manifesto was issued in 2003.[20] It differed substantially in format from the first two. Instead of presenting a reformulation of Humanist principle in detail, it attempted to sum up their fundamental concepts in a one page document of seven themes — all of which were worded in such an obfuscatory manner as to be almost unintelligible.

The document was signed by 21 Nobel Laureates. It concluded with an affirmation in the Humanist belief "that humanity has the ability to progress toward its highest ideals." And once again, it declared, "The responsibility for our lives and the kind of world in which we live is ours and ours alone."[21]

There have been other expressions of Humanism along the way. One of the most significant was "A Secular Humanist Declaration" which was issued in 1980. It was written by Paul Kurtz, who had been one of the authors of the Second Humanist Manifesto.

Paul Kurtz
(Wikimedia)

Paul Kurtz (1925-2012) is considered to be "the father of Secular Humanism."[22] He was a professor of philosophy at the State University of New York at Buffalo. In his highly lauded personal declaration, he literally let his hair down and let it be known in no-uncertain-terms that he had declared war on Christianity:[23]

> . . . . we find that traditional views of the existence of God either are meaningless, have not yet been demonstrated to be true, or are tyrannically exploitative. Secular humanists may be agnostics, atheists, rationalists or skeptics, but they find insufficient evidence for the claim that some divine purpose exists for the universe.
>
> They reject the idea that God has intervened miraculously in history or revealed himself to a chosen few or that he can save or redeem sinners. They believe that men and women are free and are responsible for their own destinies and that they cannot look toward some transcendent Being for salvation. We reject the divinity of Jesus, the divine mission of Moses, Mohammed, and other latter day prophets and saints of the various sects and denominations.

In fact, Kurtz went much further by declaring war on all religions. He listed the following groups as the enemies of Secular Humanism:[24]

- "Dogmatic authoritarian religions"

- "Fundamentalist, literalist and doctrinaire Christianity"

- "Uncompromising Moslem clericalism in the Middle East and Asia"

- "The Roman Catholic papal authority"

- "Nationalistic religious Judaism"

- "Obscurantist religions in Asia"

International Expressions of Humanism

The inaugural congress of the International Humanist and Ethical Union was held in Amsterdam in August of 1952. The Amsterdam Declaration which it issued,[25] like the First Humanist Declaration of 1933, presented Humanism as an alternative religion, calling it "a faith that answers the challenge of our times."[26] Again, such terms are an embarrassment to Humanists today since they now vehemently reject the idea that their philosophy is really just another religion of Man.

The 1952 Amsterdam Declaration was very vague and general in nature. It called for "a world-wide application of scientific method to problems of human welfare."[27] And it endorsed the fundamental idea of Humanism — that Man can save himself: "Liberated from fear [religion], the energies of man will be available for a self-realisation to which it is impossible to foresee the limit."[28]

Fifty years later, in 2002, a new Amsterdam Declaration was issued.[29] Like the Second Humanist Declaration of 1973, all references to Humanism as a religion were dropped. And like the First Amsterdam Declaration, this one was once again rather vague, consisting of seven generally worded articles.

The first began by asserting that morality should be "based on understanding and concern for others" and not on any "external sanction" (like the Bible).[30] The second article affirmed a belief in "human thought and action rather than divine intervention."[31] The rest of the articles were broad and general in nature.

The Declaration concluded by asserting confidence that "we have the means to solve the problems that confront us all."[32] And what were the means that were named? No surprises — "free inquiry, the power of science and creative imagination."[33] In other words, Man's only hope is himself.

The Impact on America

This pernicious anti-God philosophy-religion of Humanism is what has come to dominate Western civilization, including the United States. It is what has generated the culture war that has been raging in America since the mid-20th Century. It has been embraced by the media, Hollywood, our public schools, our universities and our legal system. Most important, it has become the dominant philosophy of our old mainline Protestant denominations.

The overall result has been a rapid secularization and paganization of our society to the point that we are now a nation in all-out revolt against God.

If you need any convincing of this, then get on the Internet, go to Google and type in words like Christianity, Christian and Jesus. You will be stunned at the out-right hatred that

is expressed in the articles that will pop up. The same is true if you type in the names of prominent Christian leaders like Franklin Graham.

Our nation was founded on a Judeo-Christian consensus of values. Humanists hate that consensus and have been determined to destroy it. Below is one of the classic statements of Humanist contempt for the values that made this nation great. It was written by John Dunphy and was published in *The Humanist* magazine in 1983 under the title, "A Reli-

John Dunphy
(Photo supplied by Dunphy)

gion for A New Age:"[34]

> I am convinced that the battle for human-
> kind's future must be waged and won in the
> public school classroom by teachers who cor-
> rectly perceive their role as the proselytizers of
> a new faith: a religion of humanity that recog-
> nizes the spark of what theologians call divin-
> ity in every human being. There teachers must
> embody the same selfless dedication of the
> most rabid fundamentalist preacher, for they
> will be ministers of another sort, utilizing a
> classroom instead of a pulpit to convey hu-
> manist values in whatever subject they teach,
> regardless of the educational level — pre-
> school, daycare, or large state university. The
> classroom must and will become an arena of
> conflict between the old and the new — the
> rotting corpse of Christianity, together with all
> its adjacent evils and misery, and the new faith
> of humanism, resplendent in its promise of a
> world in which the never-realized Christian
> ideal of "love thy neighbor" will finally be
> achieved.

As you can see, Dunphy is not embarrassed at all to call Secular Humanism what it really is — namely, a religion. Nor is he hesitant to make it clear that the goal of Secular Human-ism is to destroy the influence of Christianity. He also made it clear that the public school system is the means by which Humanists intend to achieve their goals.

This statement rattled Christian leaders at the time, and Dunphy took great delight in that fact. He later bragged about the statement having "all the subtlety of a charging rhino-ceros."[35]

Eleven years later, in 1994, Dunphy published a follow-up article in the *Secular Humanist Bulletin*. He reiterated his attitude and then underlined it with a victory statement:[36]

> Have I mellowed over the past 11 years? Of course, who hasn't? But have I repudiated or even questioned the basic tenets of "A Religion For A New Age"? No, nor can I envision myself ever doing so.
>
> How do I respond to the fundamentalists who are so incensed by the essay? If they have the decency to confront me to my face instead of sending anonymous hate-letters, I usually say something to the effect that Pat Buchanan was right at the 1992 Republican National Convention when he stated that a cultural civil war rages across America. While the struggle is certainly quite complex and multifaceted, I continue, a significant aspect of it is comprised of the conflict between the totalitarian Christianity of the Radical Right and the force of humanism. And then I add, "But here's something that Mr. Buchanan neglected to mention in his address: Humanism is going to win."

In 2006, Dunphy published another attack on Judeo-Christian values in the *Secular Humanist Bulletin*. It concluded with this proclamation:[37]

> I don't care to live in a nation in which Genesis will someday be uniformly taught as "creation science," abortion is criminalized, little girls are socialized for careers as housekeepers and baby machines, and homosexuality is again stigmatized as a perversion and mental illness. I don't want an America in which the cross replaces the flag as the na-

tional symbol and the Bible becomes the law
of the land.

As far back as 1930, a Humanist spokesman named
Charles F. Potter, who was a Unitarian minister, predicted
success over Christianity through the educational system. He
wrote:[38]

Education is . . . a most powerful ally of
humanism, and every American school is a
school of humanism. What can a theistic Sunday school's meeting for an hour once a week,
and teaching only a fraction of the children, do
to stem the tide of the five-day program of
humanistic teaching?

A Forgotten Heritage

We as a nation have come so far, so fast, in our capitula-
tion to Humanism that today most young people don't even
know about our nation's Judeo-Christian heritage, and for
adults under 50, it is a dim and hazy past.

Today, revisionist historians, guided by their Humanist
philosophy are working overtime to rewrite our nation's
history in order to remove all traces of the Judeo-Christian
consensus that the Declaration of Independence and our
Constitution were based upon. The result is that the average
American today is stunned to discover that our nation's
Supreme Court made the following declaration in 1892: "This
is a Christian nation. We are Christian people, and the
morality of the country is deeply engrafted upon Christianity."[39]

In 1954, Chief Justice Earl Warren, who had been appointed to the Supreme Court by President Eisenhower the
year before, was the featured speaker at a prayer breakfast in
Washington, D.C. *Time* magazine covered the event and
reported that Warren made the following comments:[40]

I believe no one can read the history of our country without realizing that the Good Book and the spirit of the Saviour have from the beginning been our guiding geniuses.

Whether we look to the first Charter of Virginia . . . or to the Charter of Massachusetts Bay . . . or to the Fundamental Orders of Connecticut . . . the same objective is present: a Christian land governed by Christian principles. . .

I believe the entire Bill of Rights came into being because of the knowledge our forefathers had of the Bible and their express belief in it . . . I like to believe we are living today in the spirit of the Christian religion. I like also to believe that as long as we do so no great harm can come to our country.

That was a little over 60 years ago. I dare say that if the current Chief Justice, John Roberts, were to make such a statement today, there would be an immediate move in Congress to impeach him on the basis that he had overstepped the boundary of "the separation of church and state."

The words, "under God," were added by Congress to our nation's Pledge of Allegiance in 1954 at the urging of President Eisenhower. Today, there are

Earl Warren
(July 1, 1957)

constant demands to remove the words, and many groups refuse to say them. It was President Ronald Reagan who stated, "America needs God more than God needs America.

If we ever forget that we are 'one nation under God,' then we will be a nation gone under."[41]

Jim Garlow, the pastor of Skyline Church in La Mesa, California, is considered to be an insightful historian of Christianity. He has presented a sweeping overview of the relationship between Bible-believing Christians and American society:[42]

1607 - 1833	—	The Establishment (236 years)
1833 - 1918	—	The Predominant Force (85 years)
1918 - 1968	—	The Sub-dominant Force (50 years)
1968 - 1988	—	A Sub-culture (20 years)
1988 - 1998	—	A Counter Culture (10 years)
1998 - 2008	—	An Antithetical Culture (10 years) (In full opposition to the predominant values of the culture)
Since 2008	—	A Persecuted Culture

This is a chilling analysis that clearly shows that Christians have lost the culture war. Notice how the changes have accelerated since the decade of the 1960s which was characterized by open rebellion against America's Judeo-Christian consensus.

Prophetic Fulfillment

Again, we have come a long way in a very short period of time. And it has all been in the wrong direction.

What we are witnessing is the

Jim Garlow
(www.skylinechurch.org)

fulfillment of a very important end time Bible prophecy that was penned by the Apostle Paul in 2 Timothy 3:

> 1) But realize this, that in the last days difficult times will come.

> 2) For men will be *lovers of self, lovers of money*, boastful, arrogant, revilers, disobedient to parents, ungrateful, unholy,

> 3) unloving, irreconcilable, malicious gossips, without self-control, brutal, haters of good,

> 4) treacherous, reckless, conceited, *lovers of pleasure* rather than lovers of God,

> 5) holding to a form of godliness, although they have denied its power; Avoid such men as these. [Emphasis added]

Notice the three things that Paul says people will love in the end times: self, money and pleasure.

The love of self is Humanism. The love of money is Materialism, and the love of pleasure is Hedonism. These three go hand-in-hand. Whenever Humanism is your religion, your god will be money and your life-style will be given over to the pursuit of pleasure.

There is a fourth element in this equation. The inevitable product of the combination of the love of self, money and pleasure is Nihilism. This is a fancy philosophical word for despair. And that is exactly where our nation is today. There are millions who are wallowing in despair as evidenced in their attempt to find meaning in life through sex, drugs, alcohol, Eastern religions and the pursuit of money, pleasure and power. This spirit of despair is what Paul sums up in the list of attitudes he says will characterize people in the end times.

The deterioration of society that we are witnessing today due to the triumph of Humanism was also prophesied by

Jesus. In His Olivet Discourse, delivered during the last week of His life, He prophesied that in the end times society would become as evil as it was in the days of Noah (Matthew 24:36-39).

If you will take a look at Genesis 6, where a description of Noah's society is provided, you will find that it was characterized by two things: immorality and violence. The world we live in today is a mirror of that corrupt society.

God's Response to American Rebellion

When we began to make the shift away from God in order to place our focus on Man, the Lord responded by raising up prophetic voices to call our nation to repentance. The purpose of this book is to identify these voices and present their messages.

The persons I have identified are not the only prophetic voices God has raised up. They simply seem to be the most anointed ones, and therefore the most significant.

I could, for example, have included someone like William F. Buckley, Jr. (1925-2008), who, at the age of 25, startled the academic world with his book, *God and Man at Yale*.[43]

In this book, published in 1951, he revealed that although Yale was founded as a Christian university, and still claimed to be one, its faculty contained atheists, agnostics and socialists. He claimed this was the trend in universities throughout the nation,

William F. Buckley, Jr.
(November 11, 1967)

and he warned that it was undercutting the Judeo-Christian heritage of our nation.

Buckley was right on target, but he was roundly condemned as a fascist who was attacking "academic freedom." Some even claimed that his criticisms were motivated by the fact that he was a Catholic who was speaking out against a Protestant university!

Since that time, nearly all our major universities, both public and private, have become bastions of Humanism. Looking back, we can clearly see that Buckley's concerns were justified and prophetic in nature.

Phyllis Schlafly (1924-2016) and Jerry Falwell (1933-2007) are other persons who I could have featured. Both were great front-line warriors in behalf of Judeo-Christian values. But I have always — rightly or wrongly — viewed them more as political operatives than prophetic voices.

As we begin to look now at the prophetic voices I have selected, we need to be reminded of two of the saddest verses in the Bible, written about another nation that, like America, was greatly blessed by God and ended up rebelling against Him. I have in mind the ancient nation of Judah.

2 Chronicles 36:15-16

15) The LORD, the God of their fathers, sent word to them again and again by His messengers, because He had compassion on His people and on His dwelling place;

16) but they continually mocked the messengers of God, despised His words and scoffed at His prophets, until the wrath of the LORD arose against His people, until there was no remedy.

Part 1
Past Voices

Peter Marshall

Chapter 1

Peter Marshall:
A Voice Calling for Commitment

How long will you hesitate between two opinions? If the LORD is God, follow Him; but if Baal, follow him. — 1 Kings 18:21

The first prophetic voice I would cite came from the heart of a great Scottish-American preacher named Peter Marshall. He came to this country in 1927 when he was 25 years old and died in 1949 when he was only 47.

During his 22 years in this country, he went to seminary in Georgia and distinguished himself as an eloquent preacher. He quickly became the pastor of the prestigious New York Presbyterian Church in Washington, D.C. in 1937 — the church that was known as "the Church of the Presidents."

In 1947 he became the Chaplain of the United States Senate. At that time, our nation was on top of the world. We had won World War II and had emerged from the war as the world's most powerful nation. Our economy had been revived and was generating unprecedented wealth. Our potential for the future seemed unlimited.[1]

But Peter Marshall was spiritually unsettled. Even before the war ended in 1945 he sensed in his soul that America was heading in the wrong direction — toward a secular, pagan society.

He unleashed his pent-up concerns in a sermon delivered in 1944 at a church in New Orleans. The sermon was titled "Trial by Fire," and it focused on the spiritual battle portrayed in the Bible between Elijah and the prophets of Baal.[2]

Trial by Fire
The message of Elijah for today.

Dr. Peter Marshall

The setting of the text is one of the most dramatic in the Old Testament. The leaders of the nation, including the king, had come together to make a great decision. It was a national emergency, something had to be done. Elijah the prophet had called them to meet on Mount Carmel to settle no less a question than whom they should worship. It was a day of choice, a day of destiny.

The cover of the LP album of Peter Marshall's recording of "Trial by Fire."

William Penn said that "Men must be governed by God or they will be ruled by tyrants." Here then was an ancient Hebrew prophet facing the very same issue, and making his people face it with him.

A Blessed Heritage

They all knew the history of their nation, how that their fathers had come out of the wilderness, out of bondage into a new land of pioneers. Behind them were great leaders — Moses and Aaron and Joshua — men who had been led by God. They had set up not a democracy, but a theocracy, a state governed by God.

The true God and His holy law had been written into the nation's constitution. The Ten Commandments had been to them a bill of rights and a declaration of dependence.

The leaders of the young nation had taken God as their king and sovereign. They had ample reason to believe, having seen it worked out in their own history, that righteousness alone exalted a nation, and that the only nation blessed was the one whose God was the Lord. They had seen it work in the past, their national history was proof. They had been taught that obedience to the laws of God was the only foundation for national greatness, liberty, and security. As long as the nation recognized God as supreme it could stand.

Moral Drift and Confusion

But something had been happening in the national life. The faith and vision of the founding fathers had faded. Moral decay had set in. There was confusion in the minds of the people. They were beginning to forget the principles that had made them a nation. They had begun to love things more than principle.

All around them paganism flourished. Their neighbors were not without god, they had gods, many of them, convenient gods, gods that could be worshiped in ways that appealed to the lower nature.

Materialism had a god, and his name was Baal. He offered to his devotees the things that human instincts crave. He was a god of the flesh. His priests encouraged the people to follow their natural inclinations. It was worship in indulgence, expressed in lust, and adored in selfishness. It had no inhibitions at all.

It said "Look after number one, be yourself, be natural." Self-expression and natural instincts was its program. A good time for everyone according to the flesh was its goal. No wonder it grew in popularity.

But still, Israel was confused. The inheritances of the past, the early teachings of their parents were not forgotten. Something of conscience was not yet drugged, and they were confused and uneasy. They took a little of Jehovah, and a little of Baal. They became by degrees more and more broad-minded. Was it not a free country? Who wanted to be old-fashioned? So morality became a relative thing.

The old absolutes were regarded as far too intolerant. The national moral standards were lowered. The worship of Baal and Jehovah got mixed somehow. It was hard to draw a line of distinction. Materialism and Idealism were often confused.

A Time for Decision

Now, Elijah saw the danger, he saw what would happen to the nation when its moral fiber was weakened. He knew the end of confusion and indecision. He believed with all his heart that national ruin and disaster were inevitable if the nation forsook Jehovah and departed from its charter and constitution. So he summoned the leaders of the country together on this day of destiny. "If the Lord be God, follow him. But if Baal, then follow him."

It was a time now for men to take sides. There was no middle ground, it could not be neutral. They had to be on one side or the other. They had to decide whether they and their nation would be governed by God, or ruled by tyrants. Elijah saw that Israel as a nation could not go with God and Baal, it had to be God or Baal.

He was a very fearless man, this Elijah. He faced the 450 prophets of Baal, the king and the nation's leaders. It had to be either or. They had to get on one side or on the other.

The Test of Gods

You remember the dramatic test of trial by fire? On the slopes of Carmel with the copper sky above them and the parched, sun-baked plains of Jezreel at their feet, the people stood waiting. Elijah announced his proposed test. Let the matter be decided once for all, let sacrifices be laid on the altar. Let him be God who would send down fire and consume the offerings.

Let Baal have the advantage of priority, let his priests have the first inning. Everything would be in their favor. The sun climbing to meridian would be at its height. There were 450 of them, and if they all prayed, that would be a lot of prayers. Let them call upon their god and let him answer if he could.

First Baal . . .

Then began the weird pagan performance with Elijah jiving at them with pointed sarcasm. While his words had blades in them, his taunts were razor-sharp. "Cry louder! Why don't you cry louder? He is a god you're crying to, isn't he? Well, he must be talking to somebody, he must be in the chase [hunting] or perhaps he's gone for a walk, peradventure he's asleep. He may be taking a nap, cry louder, wake him up."

He taunted them all day long, until they were all at the point of exhaustion. Hoarse with their shouting, wearied with their dancing, bleeding and wounded, sensing their friends are dead, they had cut themselves, hoping that the sight of their own blood spurting from tired arms and legs might cause Baal to relent and answer. They carried on until evening. But there was neither voice nor any to answer nor any that regarded.

. . . then Jehovah

Then Elijah, confident and unhurried, called the people closer. Going over to an abandoned, broken down Jehovah altar, Elijah had them set upon it a sacrifice and drenched it three times with water. He made the test more impressive by soaking the whole altar with water that ran into a trench dug all around it. And then his prayer to Jehovah, not ranting or foaming, or shouting — and its answer in fire that consumed the sacrifice, licked up the water in the trench until the people looking on cried as they fell on their faces, "The Lord, He is God! The Lord, He is God!"

The Need for Prophets

Now I suggest to you that America needs prophets today . . . who will set before the nation the essential choices . . .

A time like this demands strong minds, great hearts, true faith, and ready hands — men whom the lust of office does not kill, men whom the spoils of office cannot buy, men who possess opinions and a will, men who have honor, men who will not lie, men who can stand before a demigod and damn his treacherous flatteries without winking, tall men, sun-crowned, who live above the fog in public duty and in private thinking, while the rabble with their thumb-worn creeds, their large professions and their little deeds mingle in selfish strife.

The Danger Within

Lo, freedom weeps. Wrong rules the land. And waiting justice sleeps. We are engaged in total war and fighting for total victory. Well, it will not be won outside the United States alone. It must be won at home, as well as in Europe and in the Pacific. There are evil forces plotting within the nation as well. For men have become lovers of themselves more than lovers of their country.

All traitors are not enemy agents. Espionage and sabotage are not the only weapons that harm a war effort. Love of power and authority has enslaved the hearts of many Americans. The seeds of racial hate and intolerance have been sown. And we will reap a bitter harvest . . . Our moral standards have been lowered. And no nation makes progress in a downward direction . . .

The Message of the Hour

The old-time evangelists used to stress the tragedy of men and women individually going to hell, but we don't hear very much about that nowadays, because they say people don't believe in hell, but I notice they talk a lot about it in their conversations. But today we are living in a time when enough individuals choosing to go to hell will pull the nation down to hell with them.

The choices you make in moral and religious questions determine the way America will go. *We badly need a prophet who will have the ear of America and who will say, "If the Lord be God, follow him, but if Baal, then follow him."*

The Choices Before Us

Peter Marshall with his wife, Catherine, and their son, Peter John. (Wikipedia)

We must decide and decide quickly who is chief, whom we will serve. Millions of people in America live in moral fogs. The issues are not clear to them. They cannot face the light that makes them black or white. They want grays and neutral tints. They move in a sort of spiritual twilight.

Modified immorality on the basis of cleverness guides millions of people. Modified dishonesty within the letter of the law is the practice of millions more. Surely the time has come, because the hour is late, when we must decide. And the choice before us is plain, Jehovah or Baal. Christ or chaos. Conviction or compromise. Discipline or disintegration.

I have not stated the matter too strongly, you may agree mildly or you may disagree violently, but the time has come for us to face the duties and obligations of our citizenship and willingly to assume the disciplines imposed by the things we believe in, before we are forced to accept the disciplines of tyranny.

I, for one, am tired about hearing about our rights and privileges as American citizens. The time has come, it now is, when we ought to hear about the duties and responsibilities of our citizenship. It's just as plain and clear as that.

The Failure of the Church

The average church member has forgotten and forsaken the old disciplines. He attends service when it is convenient. His contribution of time and money is seldom such as to involve sacrifice on his part. The Church, the Word, the Sacraments have no compulsion over his life apparently.

Of course, to be honest about it, the fault is not alone that of the church member. The ministry, the church officers, are also involved in blame, because the church has failed to challenge the faith and division of the lay people in the pews. The programs of too many churches have called for neither effort nor sacrifice. All of that is sadly true.

The remedy for this sad state of affairs will lie, I believe, in the seeking of God's will for the individual church, and the adopting of a daring program for which He is challenging us all. Our strength is limited only by our faith in asking God's help. "According to your faith, be it unto you."

That is a measure that would enable us to move mountains, or if our faith be limited, cause us to stumble over mole hills. So also in the affairs of the nation. "If the Lord be God, follow him, but if Baal, then follow him."

Hypocrisy or Submission to God?

Now let us be honest about it. If we have thrown away our national heritage, if we no longer believe that this nation was founded under God, if contrary to what is stamped upon our coins, our trust is not in God but in something else, let us say so. Let us at least not be hypocrites.

A nation led by God would lead the world. The world today has many open doors, open to the gospel of Jesus Christ, peoples ready and waiting for the spiritual leadership that could steer the storm-tossed ark of humanity away from the rocks of war and the shoals of selfishness and greed.

Our own country with all its sophistication is filled with people who are hungry for the gospel. They are satiated with the materialistic philosophies that filled our stomachs and starved our souls, that supplied gadgets while they forgot God.

America's future depends upon her accepting and demonstrating God's government. If America listens to God, if America obeys God, then she can be great among all nations . . .

Knowing God's Will

We need to learn and to understand that God can guide and can control in government, in business, in labor, in management, in the home and in the heart of every individual until the whole nation is under God's control. Men can be in touch with God. In every situation men can know the will of God. They can know exactly what God wants them to do and to be. God's guidance and God's power are always available.

When men seek God they find Him and are found of Him. When men listen, God speaks. When men give God a chance, He works out His plan. He has a plan for every human life. He has a plan for you and for me. He has a plan for America, and all who truly love America will want

America to follow it. But America cannot follow it until we, until you and I as individuals, follow it.

Do you know what God wants you to do? Do you know what God wants you to be? He will tell you if you ask Him. He will speak if you give Him a chance, if you listen. It is not enough that our leaders have been guided of God. The people must be guided also. It is not enough that the minister of the church should seek to discover the will of God. The congregation likewise must discover it and follow it.

The Need for National Change

One challenge that these critical days have flung down to the church people is that we begin to be truly Christian in all our relationships, or stop pretending.

When our fighting men come back . . . they're going to be brutally frank and honest. They will see through hypocrisy. They know now the things that really count in life and they will not be deceived by this place of piety or by sham or show. They will look for changed lives, for different ways of living, for different ways of dealing with servants, with employers and with employees, different standards of value with different outlooks upon life, different dispositions.

It's a lot of nonsense what the beautifully colored advertisements are saying in old magazines, that our fighting men want to come back to an America that is totally unchanged. That is nonsense!

A Sacrifice in Vain?

The men who are on the fighting fronts now know full well, know far more clearly than they ever did before, the things in America that must be changed, if their sacrifice is to be worthwhile. We must not be the same people they left behind. We must be worthy of their sacrifices. We must be worthy of the blood that has been and will be shed. Surely the issue is crystal clear.

And they are returning now on hospital ships. They are being guided down the gang plank with bandaged eyes. They are coming creaking, swinging on creaking crutches to stand again on wounded feet on American soil. They are coming with their arms in slings, with empty sleeves tucked in tunic pockets. They are coming with trouser legs pinned up, to stand again on the America for which they fought and bled, and they are hearing in their ears, the newsboys call the headlines, "20,000 men on strike." What for? For higher wages? No, not this time. For better living conditions? No, not this time.

What then in God's name? What for? Because of strife and difference between rival labor unions. Jurisdictional disputes. Men seeking power and influence. Men seeking to exalt themselves, men seeking selfishly their own interests in a time of national crisis.

They hear of squabbles in the Senate . . . They hear — oh with what disillusionment — they hear of so many of their fellow countrymen and countrywomen who seem to be totally unaware of the issues involved.

And they look at the empty sleeves stuck in tunic pockets, they look at trouser legs pinned up to stumps of legs, they look at the wounds and the scars and the bandages, and they ask themselves, "Was it worth it? Was it worth it to storm Tarawa? Was it worth it to fly over the ash-filled skies over Berlin? Was it worth it to land at Salerno and leave a leg at Salerno?

Was it worth it to come back to a country that wants to be the same apparently, that wants to have its selfishness entrenched and encouraged and enforced? Is it worthwhile to shed your blood for people who do not seem to realize that they've got to change, that America must be worth the sacrifices that are being made for her now on every battle front. Was it worth while?"

Our Necessary Response

We must make the answer "Yes, by God it was!" We must somehow convince them, who have given up legs and arms and eyes and lives, we must convince them that it was not in vain.

Life magazine in its Christmas issue had a magnificent editorial from which I should like to quote this paragraph:[3]

> The lackadaisical days when it didn't matter much whether you were a Christian or not may be numbered. If the reassertion [of Christianity] grows strong, you may have to declare yourself more definitely than you ever expected as to whether you believe in the Word of Christ or not. This choice, if it is really forced on the Christian world, may be the choice that leads finally to the long-awaited religious revival, a revival born in the hearts of its citizens of her time, who when forced to choose, will find no truth, no comfort and no inspiration elsewhere.

We need a prophet who will have the ear of America and say to her now, "How long will you halt and stand between two opinions? If the Lord be God, follow him, but if Baal be God, follow him, *and go to hell!*"

Prayer: Oh God, bless America! May our prayer not be an empty whine of selfish pride and arrogant stupidity, but may it rather be a humble contrite plea to the God of all nations to make this land that we love so well worth defending, worth fighting for, worth dying for. Oh God help us to make America God's country. Amen.

My Response

Peter Marshall was a poetic preacher who spoke with a prophet's voice. And like all true prophets, his words continue to ring true today. In fact his sermon, "Trial by Fire," is so relevant to our day and time that it reads like it was written yesterday!

At the time he spoke these words, in 1944, our nation was involved in a World War. It was also morally adrift. The shortage of manpower on the home front had forced millions of women into the work force for the first time. In the process, women began to see their roles differently, and marriages began to crumble.

The festering sore of racism was becoming inflamed as Japanese were herded into detention camps, and minorities like Blacks and Hispanics who were discriminated against were nonetheless called upon to make the ultimate sacrifice for their country by serving in the armed forces.

Materialistic desires were being intensified by the forced rationing of all strategic goods. Labor unions were prompting strikes over matters of greed.

And the mainline Church had sold-out to the German School of Higher Criticism, accepting its argument that the Bible is Man's search for God rather than God's revelation to Man.

Like the Old Testament prophet Elijah, Dr. Marshall sensed that America was moving toward secularism, abandoning the Judeo-Christian roots that had made it great. And like Elijah, he felt the need for spiritual renewal.

He therefore called upon his parishioners, and America, to make a choice between the god of Baal (Materialism) and the true God, Jehovah. He cried out for God to empower prophetic voices who would lead the nation into spiritual revival.

Marshall could have been one of those voices if he had lived, but the Lord called him home in 1949. But before he died, the Lord had responded to his cry by raising up a new voice in Christendom who would bring revival not only to America but to people all over the world.

An Evangelistic Voice

Billy Graham
(October 25, 1954)

That new voice was not a prophetic one. Rather, it was a voice of evangelism. I'm speaking of Billy Graham. He had been an unknown youth evangelist before he was noticed by William Randolph Hearst at a youth revival in Los Angeles in 1948. Hearst was so taken by the young man's preaching, that he sent a telegram to his media empire which simply said, "Puff Graham." The next day hundreds of reporters descended upon Graham's tent meeting, and within a week, his picture was on the front page of every major American magazine.[4]

Billy Graham's ministry took off like a rocket. Millions heard the Gospel for the first time. Millions of others who had already professed Christ felt called to a re-commitment. Revival swept America and the world.

But Satan never stays on the defensive long. His counter-attack came with the cultural revolution of the 1960s and its emphasis on free sex and drugs.

Since that time, our nation has become increasingly secularized, to the point that it is unthinkable that a major American news magazine today would publish an editorial like the one Peter Marshall quotes from at the end of his sermon.

God did not ignore Peter Marshall's call for prophetic voices to speak to America. He simply waited until the appropriate time. That time came after the cultural revolution of the 1960s. In the early 1970s, God responded to Peter Marshall's plea for prophets by giving a prophetic vision to a Pentecostal preacher in New York City.

David Wilkerson

Chapter 2

David Wilkerson:
A Voice Warning America

A jealous and avenging God is the LORD;
The LORD is avenging and wrathful.
The LORD takes vengeance on His adver-
saries
And He reserves wrath for His enemies.
The LORD is slow to anger and great in
power,
And the LORD will by no means leave the
guilty unpunished. — Nahum 1:2-3

Peter Marshall spoke his concerns about the future of our nation in 1944, and just as he feared, we as a nation became captivated by materialism in the Post War Years. This obsession, in turn, fueled a spirit of rebellion against God and His Word.

For many years we had been overwhelmed by the sufferings of the Great Depression, and living through that time, we had felt a great dependency on God. But now, we were able to stand on our own, and God and His Word receded into the background.

This led to the morally disastrous decade of the 1960s and the Sexual Revolution it produced. And that, in turn, resulted in God sending us the prophetic voice that Peter Marshall had yearned for.

That voice arrived on the scene in 1974, exactly 30 years after Marshall had called for it. The voice was that of a remarkable man named David Wilkerson.

David Wilkerson

Wilkerson started out as a Pentecostal preacher in rural Pennsylvania.

In 1958, at age 27, he felt the Lord's leading to pull up stakes and move to New York City to minister to its violent street gangs. Through many trials and tears, he succeeded in establishing a ministry to the gangs, and in 1962 he published a book about his experiences which was titled, *The Cross and the Switchblade.*[1] It made him nationally famous, and even more so when it was converted into a movie in 1970.[2]

The Vision

As a result of the book and the movie, Wilkerson became the darling of the Pentecostal and Charismatic Movements — until he published another book in 1974 called *The Vision.*[3] It was advertised by the publisher as "A terrifying prophecy of Doomsday that is starting to happen now."

This book presented a very negative prophecy about the future of our nation, warning that because of our rebellion against God, we were headed toward major judgments and ultimate destruction.

Dave Wilkerson arrives in New York City in 1958.
(Wikipedia)

The world, as would be expected, wrote the book off as "insane." But what proved tragic is that the Church also dismissed the book as the ravings of a radical.

The Pentecostal and Charismatic Movements responded with strong condemnation. They were full of pillow prophets at the time who were prophesying a great end time revival that would renew and refresh America as a Christian nation. They did not want to hear a negative message from anyone, especially from their best known spokesman.

Accordingly, Wilkerson became a pariah overnight. His books were removed from the church bookstores, and he was personally condemned as a "fear-monger."

In like manner, mainline churches — both Evangelical and non-Evangelical — also denounced the book, arguing that Wilkerson must be a "false prophet" because "God no longer speaks in visions."

Wilkerson had anticipated this response because he addressed it at the beginning of his book by pointing out that the Scriptures say that in the end times, God will give His servants visions and dreams. Here is the passage from Joel chapter 2:

> 28) "It will come about after this that I will pour out My Spirit on all mankind; and your sons and daughters will prophesy, your old men will dream dreams, your young men will see visions.

> 29) "Even on the male and female servants I will pour out My Spirit in those days."

Notice verse 28 says, "It will come about *after this* . . ." After what? The previous verses indicate that it will be after the re-establishment of the nation of Israel.

In accordance with this passage in Joel, Wilkerson revealed that his prophecy for America had come from a vision given to him in April of 1973, and for that reason, he titled the book, *The Vision.*

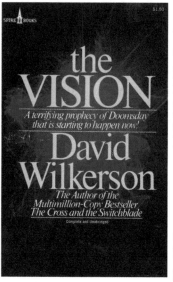

Wilkerson also pointed out at the beginning of his book that he did not believe that most of the prophecies in his vision would be fulfilled in his lifetime, and that proved true when he was tragically killed in an auto accident in East Texas in 2011.[4]

A Review of Wilkerson's Prophecies

However, many of the prophecies contained in his vision have been fulfilled since 1974. Let me give you an overview of them.

His first category was **"Worldwide Economic Confusion."** He wrote:[5]

> It is not really a depression I see coming — but a recession of such magnitude that it will affect the lifestyle of nearly every wage earner in America and around the world.

This, of course, was fulfilled in the outbreak of the Great Recession in 2008.

Wilkerson further asserted that "some of the nation's major corporations will declare bankruptcy."[6] This began in 2001 with Enron and PG&E, California's largest utility company. Ten more huge corporations collapsed during the Great Recession, including such giants as Lehman Brothers, General Motors and American Airlines. In fact the 12 largest bankruptcies in U.S. history have occurred since 2001.

Wilkerson predicted that the recession would have major political ramifications: "Fear generated by the economy will lead to a revolution at the polls."[7] This is precisely what happened when the stock market crashed in September of 2008 and Barack Obama was elected in November.

Wilkerson further predicted that because of the recession, "The auto industry is going to be hurt badly."[8] This was fulfilled when the government took over both Chrysler and General Motors during the Great Recession.

Concerning gold, Wilkerson predicted that "the price of gold is going to rise astronomically but will not be sustained over a long period of time."[9] When Wilkerson published his book in 1974, the price of gold was $183 per ounce. At the end of 2014 it was $1200 per ounce.

Wilkerson's last economic related prophecy was this:[10]

> A revived Roman Empire will eventually become the power base for a super world leader who will arise to restore economic order.

This has been partially fulfilled in the formation of the European Union which became a supranational political organization in 1992 with the Treaty of Maastricht.

Wilkerson's second category of predictions related to what he called **"Drastic Weather Changes and Earthquakes."** He summed it up by saying:[11]

> The world had best prepare for weather changes that cannot be explained by any other word but 'supernatural.' The world is about to witness the beginnings of great sorrows brought about by history's most drastic weather changes, earthquakes, floods — terrible calamities . . .

As you can see from the chart on the next page, worldwide weather-related disasters have increased from an average of 300 per year in the 1980s to almost 1,000 per year in 2010.

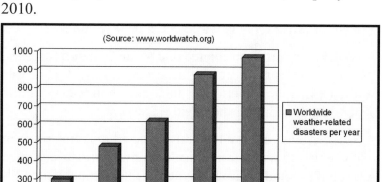

The third category of predictions in Wilkerson's vision he labeled **"A Flood of Filth."** Again, keep in mind that he was writing in 1974:[12]

> We are facing a moral landslide . . . Satan is going to open the floodgates of Hell and seek to baptize the world in erotic filth, smut and sensuality.

The evidence of this is all around us and in our homes through the invasion of television filth. And the corruption of entertainment is exactly what Wilkerson predicted: "Movies and TV programs will feature the exploitation of every sex theme, with an emphasis on blood, violence and occult practices."[13] Movies like *Pulp Fiction* and television programs like *Criminal Minds* are doing this today.

Further, Wilkerson warned that "there will be movies glamorizing rape."[14] The recent film, *50 Shades of Grey* just did this. He also predicted that "thousands of newsstands across the nation will soon be selling explicit sex magazines that will make *Playboy* seem almost puritanical."[15] This, has become a reality with the publication of sleazy magazines like *Quicky, ADHD Sex, Carnival* and *Hustler.*

Wilkerson declared that "students will be told that homosexual love is normal."[16] In recent years several school systems all over the nation have incorporated teaching units designed to portray homosexuality as normal — even at the elementary school level. This effort has even infiltrated books and magazines aimed at children.

Again, keep in mind that Wilkerson wrote about his vision in 1973, and the book was published in 1974. Continuing with his focus on homosexuality, he asserted: "The homosexual community will become so militant and brazen that they will flaunt their sin on network talk shows."[17] Just tune into the late night interview programs or any afternoon to Ellen DeGeneres' show and you will witness the fulfillment of this prophecy.

In the Church world, Wilkerson predicted that "homosexuals and lesbians will be ordained and given places of authority."[18] The Episcopal Church elected its first homosexual bishop in 2003, and since that time, many of the mainline denominations have sanctioned the ordination of practicing homosexuals.

Commenting further on the Church, Wilkerson asserted: "Divorce and immorality will become more and more commonplace among ministers."[19] This problem was featured on the cover of *Time* magazine in April of 1987 when the magazine focused on the problems of Jimmy Swaggart and also commented on the controversies surrounding Jim and Tammy Bakker.

Wilkerson's fourth category was **"Problems with Youth."** Since this had always been the focus of his ministry, he had more predictions in this category than any other. To summarize:

- He said he saw youth hating their parents and rebelling against them, even to the point of betraying their parents.[20]

- He saw them enslaved to alcohol and drugs and predicted the legalization of Marijuana.[21]

- All of which would be magnified by an astronomical divorce rate.[22]

Wilkerson's fifth and last category of prophecies contained in his vision was what he called **"Persecution Madness."** He predicted the growing persecution of Christian believers:[23]

> I see an hour of persecution coming such as mankind has never before witnessed. This will be a persecution of true Jesus believers that will soon arise like a many-headed monster out of the sea.

Wilkerson even predicted that Christian harassment would become official government policy:[24]

> An antichrist spirit will enter the hearts of certain men in high places in government and in the judicial system, causing these officials to engage in legal maneuvers designed to harass independent churches, missionaries and ministers.

We can see this antichrist spirit operating at all governmental levels today.

Wilkerson stated that the entertainment industry would focus on demeaning portrayals of Christians and Christianity, and would blaspheme all that is sacred:[25]

> TV comedy shows will become bolder and bolder in poking fun at Christ and true Christians . . . Television programming will

become absolutely blasphemous . . .

Need I bother to say this has been fulfilled?

Unfulfilled Prophecies

And yet, despite the fulfillment of these very specific pro-phecies contained in Wilkerson's vision, some have contin-ued to claim he was a "false prophet" because some of his predictions have not yet been fulfilled.

But the same could be said of Isaiah, Jeremiah, Ezekiel and Daniel because all of them made prophecies 2,500 years ago that still have not been fulfilled. How do we know they are not false prophets? Because they made prophecies about their day and time that were fulfilled and they also made prophecies about the first coming of the Messiah that were fulfilled. So we can be confident that their unfulfilled prophe-cies concerning the end times will also be fulfilled.

The Bible says the test of a prophet is whether or not his prophecies come true (Jeremiah 28:9): ". . . when the word of the prophet comes to pass, then that prophet will be known as one whom the Lord has truly sent."

Thus, if I were to prophesy that America will be de-stroyed by a nuclear attack, you would have to wait until our nation was destroyed to determine whether or not I was a false prophet — and you might have to wait several hundred years.

But, if I were to say America will be destroyed by a nuclear attack before January 1, 2016, and that did not happen, then you would know I am a false prophet.

Wilkerson did not give dates for any of the prophecies in his vision, except to say that all the predictions would not be fulfilled in his lifetime. Therefore, it is impossible to declare him to be a "false prophet" at this point in time.

Some of the unfulfilled prophecies are very ominous. They include:

- The U.S. will experience the worst earthquake in its history in a place least expected.[26]

- The taxation of churches, ministries and Christian schools will be instituted.[27]

- TV will feature full nudity and X-rated porno movies.[28]

The Point of No Return

But for me, the most ominous statement in his book was this one:[29]

I believe we have passed the point of no return.

Again, that was 1974.

I underlined that statement in red and put a question mark after it. That's because I was not ready to say that in 1974. *I am now.*

The Bible clearly teaches there is a "point of no return" when a nation is in rebellion against God. It is the tipping point where God decides to deliver the nation from remedial judgments to complete destruction. In the Bible it is referred to as "when the wound becomes incurable" (Jeremiah 30:12).

I will cover this concept in detail in chapter 14.

Conclusion

David Wilkerson was a modern day prophet of God who boldly declared an unpopular message that no one wanted to hear — neither believers nor unbelievers. He was written off as a quack.

But time has validated his message and God's grace in giving it to us. We cannot say that we were not warned. Unfortunately, we turned a deaf ear to Wilkerson's warning, and God has since raised up other voices in His effort to get our attention.

Jeremiah 30:12-14

12) "For thus says the LORD, *'Your wound is incurable* and your injury is serious.

13) 'There is no one to plead your cause; no healing for your sore, no recovery for you.

14) 'All your lovers have forgotten you, they do not seek you; for I have wounded you with the wound of an enemy, with the punishment of a cruel one, because your iniquity is great and your sins are numerous.'"

Francis Schaeffer

Chapter 3

Francis Schaeffer:
A Voice Advocating
A Biblical Worldview

And do not be conformed to this world, but be transformed by the renewing of your mind, so that you may prove what the will of God is, that which is good and acceptable and perfect. — Romans 12:2

At the end of his life in 1984, at age 72, Francis Schaeffer had established himself as the leading Christian spokesman against theological Modernism, philosophical Humanism and political Pragmatism. On the positive side, he had become Christendom's foremost spokesman in behalf of a Christian worldview.

- U.S. Surgeon General, Dr. C. Everett Koop, called him, "God's man for the era."[1]

- Billy Graham said of him, "He was truly one of the great evangelical statesmen of our generation . . . More than virtually any other thinker, he had a keen insight into the major theological and philosophical battles of our time"[2]

- President Ronald Reagan wrote to his family, "He will long be remembered as one of the great Christian thinkers of our century."[3]

- *Time* magazine described him as "a missionary to intel-lectuals."[4]

- Schaeffer said of himself, "I really am a country preacher. But I had to develop my philosophy to speak to a world that no longer believes that truth exists."[5]

Francis Schaeffer spent his life advocating a Christian worldview. In the process he fiercely defended the inerrancy of the Scriptures and the existence of God. He also pro-claimed the sanctity of human life and constantly warned the Western World about the dangers of Humanism.

Much of what he had to say was highly theological and philosophical in nature and difficult to comprehend, but in his final years, he brought his message down to earth through books and documentary films that were aimed at the lay-person.

Early Life

Francis August Schaeffer, IV was born in 1912 in Ger-mantown, Pennsylvania. Neither of his parents were Chris-tians, and neither of them were well educated. His father was a common laborer with only a third grade education.

Francis became a Christian at age 17 after his interest in Greek philosophy ultimately led him to read the Bible. Later in life, he observed: "What rang the bell for me was the answers in Genesis, and that with these you had answers — real answers — and without these there were no answers either in philosophy or in the religion I had heard preached."[6]

When he told his parents of his plan to attend Hampden-Sydney College in Virginia in order to study for the ministry, they strongly opposed the idea. But he went anyway, not knowing how he would be able to afford it.[7] The college was an all-male school affiliated with the Presbyterian Church.

At the end of his freshman year in 1932, Francis met the woman who would become his wife. She was Edith Seville, who was a student at Beaver College for Women in Pennsylvania. Both had returned home for the summer, and they met at the Presbyterian church where they were attending.

Edith had radically different background. Both of her parents were college graduates and were Christian missionaries to China, where Edith was born. She was two years younger than Francis.

Despite the fact that Francis had a hot temper and Edith had a strong will, they fell in love and were married in 1935.[8] One of the key elements that drew them together was the fact that both were Fundamentalists who strongly believed in the inerrancy of the Scriptures.

Francis proceeded on to the newly established Faith Theological Seminary in Wilmington, Delaware, from which he graduated in 1938.[9] He then became the first graduate to be ordained in the Bible Presbyterian Church, a new denomination that had broken away from the Orthodox Presbyterian Church over the issue of inerrancy.[10]

Early Ministry

After spending nine years pastoring Bible Presbyterian churches in Pennsylvania and Missouri, the denomination's foreign missions board sent Francis on a three-month trip to Europe to build a network among "Bible-believing" churches and pastors.[11] He quickly discovered that the European churches were caught up in apostasy.[12]

After reporting back to the missions board about what he had discovered in Europe, the board decided to send him and his wife to Europe as missionaries. So, in 1948, they departed the States and settled in Lausanne, Switzerland.

Shortly before their departure, one of their daughters became seriously ill and required surgery at Philadelphia Children's Hospital. Her surgeon was Dr. C. Everett Koop, who had just become a Christian a few weeks before. The Schaeffers hit it off with Dr. Koop, and they became life-long friends, laying the groundwork for a very important collaboration that would take place 29 years later in 1977.[13]

Three years after his move to Switzerland, Schaeffer experienced a crisis of faith during which he "rethought everything."[14] The experience proved to be a major turning point in his life. He emerged from it with a complete and strong reaffirmation of his faith.

His biographer, Louis Gifford Parkhurst, Jr., states that Francis came out of the struggle "with the firm conviction that God is truly, objectively *there* whether we think He is or not, that the Bible is true in all that it affirms, that the Bible applies to the whole of life, and that the spiritual reality of the love and holiness of the Holy Spirit must be present in our lives, especially so while fighting for the truth."[15]

L'Abri Fellowship

In 1955, the Schaeffers moved to Huémoz, Switzerland and established a ministry called L'Abri Fellowship. The name, L'Abri, is French for "The Shelter." It quickly became a spiritual community that attracted young college students from all over Europe, many of whom were caught up in Existential philosophy and were desperately searching for some meaning in life.

In the years that followed, as he worked with these young people, Francis developed and fine-tuned his arguments against Humanism. He did the same with his arguments in defense of the Christian faith. His lectures were recorded, and then the recordings were transcribed into books that began to be published in 1968. The books resulted in invitations to speak at universities around the world.

Schaeffer's Overview

In 1974, Schaeffer began work on a book and a ten part film that would bring him to widespread attention among American Evangelicals. The project was called *How Should We Then Live?*[16] It was an in-depth study of the rise and decline of Western thought and culture, presented from a Christian worldview.

Beginning with the Roman Empire, Schaeffer explained how a Humanist belief in Man led to a society devoid of any standard of right and wrong, resulting in a moral rottenness that ultimately destroyed the Empire from within.

During the Middle Ages (500 to 1500 AD), the theology of Thomas Aquinas (1225-1274) resulted in the distortion of Christianity because he argued that the Fall of Man had only corrupted Mankind's will, but not his intellect. Therefore, truth could be perceived through reason, and the Church began to mix Scripture with the ideas of non-Christian philosophers like Aristotle. Increasingly, Man became the center of religion and the decisions of the Pope and Church Councils began to replace the authority of the Scriptures.

The Renaissance (1300 to 1700) propelled Humanism to the center of all intellectual activity, including the arts. This movement began in southern Europe, focused in Italy, and gradually spread to all the continent. It served as a bridge from the Middle Ages to modern history. Man was placed at the center of all things and was glorified in the arts — as with Michelangelo's statue that was titled *David.* Concerning this artistic masterpiece, Schaeffer observed:[17]

> Michelangelo took a piece of marble so flawed that no one thought it could be used, and out of it he carved this overwhelming statue. But let us notice that the *David* was not the Jewish David of the Bible. *David* was simply a title. Michelangelo knew his Judaism, and in the statue the figure is not circumcised. We are not to think of this as the biblical David but as the humanistic ideal. Man is great!

But in northern Europe there was a retreat from Humanism that was motivated by the Reformation that began in 1517. God and His Word were propelled back into the center

Francis Schaeffer in 1974 at age 62.
(http://engagingmedia.info)

of the Church and society. Once again, Man's fallenness was recognized, but at the same time, there was a renewed emphasis on the dignity of Man as created in the image of God.

Schaeffer pointed out that both the Renaissance and the Reformation produced greater freedom for people, but whereas the Reformation led to responsible freedom, the Renaissance produced an irresponsible freedom of license because, being grounded in Humanism, there was no basis for morality.

This inherent problem with Humanism was demonstrated in the 18th Century in France with the rise of what came to be called, "The Enlightenment." The French philosopher, Voltaire (1694-1778) argued for a society based on reason rather than faith or Catholic doctrines. Schaeffer observed: "To the Enlightenment thinkers, man and society were perfectible."[18] The French proclaimed the "Goddess of Reason" and committed themselves to a thoroughly secular society. The result was the bloodbath of the French Revolution (1789-1799) which led to the authoritarian rule of Napoleon Bonaparte.

Meanwhile, a Scientific Revolution had started with the Polish astronomer, Copernicus (1473-1543) who formulated a model of the universe that placed the sun rather than the earth at the center of the universe.

Both the Renaissance and the Reformation helped to fuel the increasing emphasis on the scientific method — the Renaissance through its emphasis on reason and the Reformation through its insistence that we live in an ordered universe of natural laws created by God. Many of the leading scientists were Christians, including such people as Francis Bacon (1561-1626), Blaise Pascal (1623-1662), Isaac Newton (1643-1727), and Michael Faraday (1791-1867).

But this Christian base did not last long as Charles Darwin (1809-1882) and others like him with a Humanist worldview began to push God aside, elevate human reason and convert Mankind into an accident of evolution living in the midst of a meaningless universe.

All of which produced what Schaeffer called "The Age of Fragmentation," when both philosophers and artists began to view life as an "absurdity."[19] All is chance. There is no purpose. Both the world and Man have become fragmented. There is no right or wrong. God is dead.

This radical shift in which all of God's creation is viewed as nothing more than an accidental machine, including people, led to the horrors the 20th Century: the Communist Revolution, the Nazi Holocaust, the Chinese Cultural Revolution and the Cambodian Genocide.

These atrocities illustrated a point Schaeffer made when he wrote: "If the unsaved man was consistent, he would be an atheist in religion, an irrationalist in philosophy . . . and completely amoral in the widest sense."[20] And so it came to be.

The American Application

In both the ending of the book and the film, Schaeffer brought all this home to the United States in what he called "The Age of Personal Peace and Affluence." By the time of the mid-20th Century the erosion of a Christian consensus in America had produced a population where a majority of the people had adopted "two impoverished values" — "personal peace and affluence." He explained his observation as follows:[21]

> Personal peace means just to be left alone, not to be troubled by the troubles of other people . . . Personal peace means wanting to have my personal life pattern undisturbed in my lifetime, regardless of what the result will be in the lifetimes of my children and grandchildren. Affluence means an overwhelming and ever-increasing prosperity — a life made up of things, things and more things — a success judged by an ever-higher level of material abundance.

According to Schaeffer, these two predominant post-war secular values produced the cultural revolt of the 1960s, as young people decided there must be more to life than selfishness and greed. As Schaeffer put it, "They were right in their analysis of the problem, but they were mistaken in their solutions" — mainly Hedonism as expressed in drugs and sex.[22]

Schaeffer concluded by speaking prophetically about our society. He said, "As the memory of the Christian consensus which gave us freedom within the biblical form increasingly is forgotten, a manipulating authoritarianism will tend to fill the vacuum."[23] Specifically, he warned of rule by an arbitrary elite with arbitrary values.

He also warned of three future dangers:[24]

1) Genetic tinkering with human beings.

2) Manipulation by the media, particularly television.

3) Reliance on sociological law — that is, law not based on the Bible or Natural Law or the Constitution, but law based on shifting public opinion.

The final statement in his book was an ominous one: "This book is written in the hope that this generation may turn from that greatest wickedness, the placing of any created thing in the place of the Creator, and that this generation may get its feet out of the paths of death and may live."[25]

The book, *How Should We Then Live?* was published in 1976. The film based on the book was released in 1977. Seminars featuring the film were held all across America in 1977 and 1978. In October of 1978 Schaeffer was diagnosed with lymphoma cancer, and he began treatments at the Mayo Clinic in Rochester, Minnesota.

His Collaboration with Koop

Meanwhile, he continued working on a new book and film in collaboration with his old friend, Dr. C. Everett Koop (1916-2013). Later, in 1982 Dr. Koop became President Reagan's Surgeon General. This new book was titled, *Whatever Happened to the Human Race?*[26] Both the book and the film were released in 1979.

The book began with a powerful dedication that read: "To those who were robbed of life, the unborn, the weak, the sick, the old, during the dark ages of madness, selfishness, lust and greed for which the last decades of the twentieth century are remembered."[27] This book and film focused on the abominations of abortion, infanticide and euthanasia, as practiced in America at that time.

The first sentence in the book summed up its thesis: "Cultures can be judged in many ways, but eventually every nation in every age must be judged by this test: *how did it treat people?*"[28] The authors continued with this observation: "The reason we are writing this book is that we feel strongly that we stand today on the edge of a great abyss."[29] They then zeroed-in on the reason for this crisis:[30]

> The Christian consensus held that neither the majority nor an elite is absolute. God gives standards of value, and His absolutes are binding on both the ordinary person and those in all places of authority . . . because the Christian consensus has been put aside, we are faced today with a flood of personal cruelty.

The book proceeds to present a passionate, logical and biblical case against abortion, with the warning that it will lead to the acceptance of both infanticide and euthanasia. In the process, they provide many horrifying examples of the practice of infanticide and euthanasia among the medical profession, although neither was legal at that time.

They point out how we as a nation are being reconditioned in our thinking to accept infanticide. After all, what is the difference in killing a baby a few minutes before birth or a few minutes after? Both are murder. And if parents can pay to have their children killed, what is going to prevent children from paying to have their parents killed? "Within [the Humanist] worldview there is no room for believing that a human being has any final distinct value above that of an animal or of nonliving matter. People are merely a different arrangement of molecules."[31]

With the publication of this book, Schaeffer crossed the line between the realm of philosophy and theology into the world of social action. He and Koop concluded the book with detailed instructions about what people can do to support the sanctity of life and to vigorously oppose abortion, infanticide and euthanasia.[32]

Schaeffer's Manifesto

Despite his ongoing treatment for cancer, Schaeffer continued to write. In 1981 he published *A Christian Manifesto*.[33] It was very specifically aimed at the American landscape and the political developments that seemed to be leading the nation toward destruction. Basically, it dealt with the question of "what is the Christian's responsibility to government, law and civil disobedience?"[34]

The book was written in direct response to the *Communist Manifesto* of 1848, the *Humanist Manifesto I* of 1933 and the *Humanist Manifesto II* of 1973 — all of which placed Man at the center of all things and made him the measure of all things.[35] In contrast, Schaeffer affirmed the biblical view of Man made in the image of God with "real humanness."[36]

Schaeffer showed how our nation was originally based upon a Christian consensus that recognized the dignity of Man and the sanctity of life, while realizing that Man is fallen and therefore must be restrained through a government of checks and balances and separation of powers.[37]

He then proceeded to show that the foundations of our legal and governmental systems have eroded to the point where "secularized, sociological law" now reigns supreme.[38]

Regarding this point, he referenced a statement by the former Chief Justice of the Supreme Court, Frederick Vinson (1890-1953) who wrote: "Nothing is more certain in modern society than the principle that there are no absolutes."[39]

Schaeffer explained that "sociological law" — or what could be called "situational law" — is operational when the courts make decisions that are divorced from a standard like biblical or constitutional principles. Instead, the courts base their decisions on what is thought to be best for society.

As an example Schaeffer pointed to the Supreme Court's abortion decision in 1973. He asserted that it was a classic example of highly subjective legal decision making.[40] It was a totally arbitrary decision forced upon the majority by an elite without any constitutional basis and in complete contradiction of God's Word. (The same, of course could be said of the Court's equally arbitrary ruling in the same-sex marriage case 43 years later in 2016.)

Schaeffer launched into a detailed discussion of the relationship of Christians to their government. He affirmed the biblical teaching that we are to respect and obey our rulers.[41] But he hastened to emphasize that there are biblical limits to obedience. "The bottom line," he asserted, "is that at a certain point there is not only the right, but the duty, to disobey the state."[42] And when is that? "Any government that commands what contradicts God's Law abrogates its authority."[43]

Schaeffer concluded his manifesto by pointing out that Humanism is "an exclusivist, closed system which shuts out all contending viewpoints — especially if those views teach anything other than relative values and standards . . . As a result, the humanistic, material-energy, chance world view is completely intolerant . . ."[44] He therefore concludes:[45]

> It is not too strong to say that we are at war,
> and there are no neutral parties in the struggle.
> One either confesses that God is the final

authority, or one confesses that Caesar is Lord.

One very fascinating thing about Schaeffer's manifesto is what he had to say about the presidential election of 1980 in which Ronald Reagan was triumphant. Writing in 1981 during the first year of Reagan's presidency, he refers to it as "a unique open window" for our nation to roll back the tide of Humanism.[46] He warned that "we must beware of letting a foolish triumphalism cause us to think that all is now won and certain,"[47] because the Humanists "are deeply entrenched."[48]

Speaking prophetically, Schaeffer then concluded that if we were unable to stem the tide of Humanism during the Reagan open window, it would most likely continue to be advanced in the future through the courts.[49]

> Under the guise of 'civil liberties' . . . the Humanist forces have used the courts rather than the legislatures because the courts are not subject to the people's thinking and expression by the election process — and especially they (the courts) are not subject to re-election.[50]

The Last Book

Schaeffer concluded his life's work the way he began it, by condemning the Church for its apostasy. His message was contained in a book published in 1984, three months before his death. The book was titled, *The Great Evangelical Disaster.*[51]

In 1948, as he and his wife were preparing to move to Europe, Schaeffer had written an essay titled, "Revolutionary Christianity," in which he argued that the true revolutionary version of Christianity was not the popular "socialized gospel" of that day, but the "historic, Bible-believing Christianity that believes the task of the Church is to preach Christ and Him crucified and that men are justified by faith."[52]

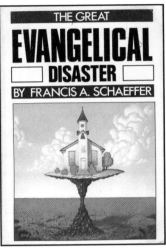

He renewed this theme in his last book. He asserted that just as the mainline denominations had been corrupted in the 1920s and 1930s by their abandonment of Scripture, the same thing was occurring in the 1970s and 1980s among Evangelicals.

He proclaimed that "the great evangelical disaster" was "the failure of the evangelical world to stand for truth as truth." And then he bluntly stated, "There is only one word for this — namely, accommodation: the evangelical church has accommodated to the world spirit of the age."[53]

How exactly? In two ways. First, Schaeffer identified the accommodation on Scripture, "so that many who call themselves Evangelicals hold a weakened view of the Bible and no longer affirm the truth of all the Bible teaches — truth not only in religious matters but in the areas of science and history and morality."[54] The second area has been on moral issues, "with no clear stand being taken even on matters of life and death."[55]

Schaeffer strongly castigated Evangelical leaders for waffling on the issue of the inerrancy of the Scriptures, "so that the full authority of Scripture is completely undercut."[56] Here's how he summarized the issue:[57]

> Unless the Bible is without error, not only
> when it speaks of salvation matters, but also
> when it speaks of history and the cosmos, we
> have no foundation for answering questions

concerning the existence of the universe and its form and the uniqueness of man. Nor do we have any moral absolutes, or certainty of salvation, and the next generation of Christians will have nothing on which to stand.

When the book was published, many responded by declaring that Schaeffer had "overstated his case."[58] But looking back at it today, some 30 years later, it is obvious that his observations were right on the mark. For today, we have Evangelical leaders who are literally denying many of the fundamentals of the faith.

Schaeffer was so disgusted with the Evangelical Movement that he declared he would no longer refer to himself as an Evangelical. Instead, he would call himself "a Bible-believing Christian."[59]

Conclusion

Francis Schaeffer was graduated to his eternal reward on May 15, 1984, at his home in Rochester, Minnesota. He was 72 years old.

The day before he died, he prayed, "Dear Father God, I have finished my work. Please take me home. I am tired."[60]

Aleksandr Solzhenitsyn

Chapter 4

Aleksandr Solzhenitsyn: A Voice Pleading For Remembrance

> *Can a virgin forget her ornaments*
> *Or a bride her attire?*
> *Yet My people have forgotten Me*
> *Days without number.*
> (Jeremiah 2:32)

Aleksandr Solzhenitsyn spoke like an Old Testament prophet when he warned America and all the Western world that it was imperiled because it had forgotten God. It proved to be a message that people did not want to hear. Accordingly, Solzhenitsyn died as a prophet without honor.

Solzhenitsyn was a Russian novelist, historian and short story writer who was born in 1918. He was an outspoken critic of the Soviet Union and Communism, and he helped raise global awareness of the inhumanity of the Soviet regime.

Solzhenitsyn grew up in poverty. His father was killed in a hunting accident shortly after his wife's pregnancy was confirmed. Solzhenitsyn's mother never remarried. She was an educated woman, and she encouraged her son's literary and scientific education. She also raised him in the Russian Orthodox faith.

His War Experiences and Arrest

During World War II, Solzhenitsyn served as an officer in the Red Army. He began to develop growing doubts about the moral foundation of the Soviet government when he witnessed repeated war crimes by the Soviet army against German civilians. Elderly people were tortured and looted, and young girls were gang raped to death.

In February of 1945, while serving in East Prussia, Solzhenitsyn was arrested for writing derogatory comments in personal letters about Stalin and his conduct of the war. He was charged with "anti-Soviet propaganda" and was sentenced to an eight year term in a labor camp.

Solzhenitsyn's prison photo.
(Wikipedia)

During the next eight years, he was transferred from one forced-labor camp to another throughout what he labeled as "The Gulag Archipelago." This gave him firsthand observations within the Soviet system for political prisoners. His experiences during this time served as the basis for his novella, *One Day in the Life of Ivan Denisovich*.[1]

In March of 1953, after his prison sentence ended, Solzhenitsyn was forced into internal exile in northeastern Kazakhstan. He was diagnosed with a cancerous tumor and almost died before the tumor went into remission. It was this experience that served as the basis for his novel, *Cancer Ward*, which was published in 1968.[2]

Solzhenitsyn's terrible experiences in the Gulag convinced him to completely abandon Marxism, and he began to return gradually to his early Christian faith.

The Thawing of Russia

In 1956, Nikita Khrushchev delivered his famous "secret speech" to a closed session of the 20th Congress of the Communist Party of the Soviet Union. In the speech, Khrushchev denounced Stalin as a brutal leader and then proceeded to provide a litany of many of his crimes.

This speech launched a period of "de-Stalinization" that included a thaw in the censorship of literature. As a result, Solzhenitsyn was freed from exile. He took a position as a secondary school math teacher and continued his research and writing about the Gulag.

His First Publications

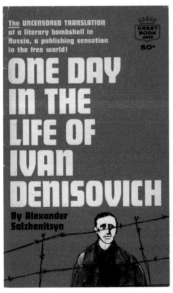

In 1962, at age 44, his short story, *One Day in the Life of Ivan Denisovich,* was published in *Novy Mir* magazine with the personal approval of Khrushchev who later defended his decision by declaring: "There's a Stalinist in each of you; there's even a Stalinist in me. We must root out this evil."[3]

The story caused a sensation and was subsequently published in book form. It became an immediate bestseller in both the Soviet Union and the West. It was the only book by Solzhenitsyn to be published in his native country, because after Khrushchev was ousted from power two years later, the censors once again clamped down on anti-Soviet writings. However, between 1962 and 1964, he did publish three short stories in Russian magazines. His next two novels, *In The First Circle* and *Cancer Ward*, and a play, *The Prisoner and the Camp Hooker,* were all published abroad in 1968.[4]

In 1970, Solzhenitsyn was awarded the Nobel Prize in Literature. He refused to travel to Stockholm to receive the award because he feared that the Soviet authorities would not allow him to return to Russia. The award cited him "for the ethical force with which he has pursued the indispensable traditions of Russian literature."[5]

His Historical Blockbuster

Solzhenitsyn's most famous book, and his tour de force, was *The Gulag Archipelago,* written between 1958 and 1967 and published in France (in Russian) in 1973.[6] It was a three-volume, seven part detailed historical exposé of the Soviet forced-labor prison system.

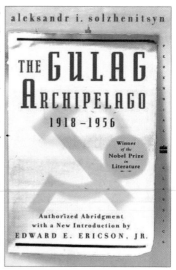

The book quickly became one of the most influential publications of the 20th Century. It has since sold over 30 million copies in 35 languages. The book was not published in the Soviet Union but was vehemently attacked by the government controlled press. In the West it was hailed as a masterpiece. George F. Kennan, the influential U.S. diplomat, called the book "the most powerful single indictment of a political regime ever to be levied in modern times."[7]

The word, GULAG, in the title of the book is an acronym for the Russian name of the bureaucracy that governed the Soviet labor camp system of prisons. The word, archipelago, was used by Solzhenitsyn to portray this system because the camps were spread across Russia like a vast "chain of islands."

The publication of this book was the last straw for the Soviet government. In September of 1974, Solzhenitsyn was arrested and deported. In the process, he was stripped of his Soviet citizenship, becoming a stateless person. He went first to Cologne, Germany and then to Zurich, Switzerland. In 1975, Stanford University invited him to move there where he lived on campus before deciding to move to Cavendish, Vermont in 1976. He remained there until 1994 when he returned to Russia.

The Speech That Stunned the Western World

Solzhenitsyn's first public speech in the United States was delivered in June of 1978, three years after his arrival. The occasion was the commencement ceremony at Harvard University where he was granted an honorary degree. He arrived on campus as a hero; he departed as a pariah.

Solzhenitsyn at Harvard in June 1978.
(www.haciendapub.com)

The Harvard intelligentsia was outraged over his presentation, and some actually booed him! *The New York Times* declared him to be a "dangerous zealot."[8] *The Washington Post* wrote him off as a man who did not understand Western society.[9] Critics denounced him as a "Tsarist reactionary, an Orthodox Christian ayatollah, a hater of democracy [and] a

Russian ultranationalist."[10] None of which were true. As one of his biographers, Daniel J. H. Mahoney, has put it: "Solzhenitsyn wasn't just dismissed; he was demonized."[11]

What in the world had Solzhenitsyn done to provoke such outrage? The answer is simple. He spoke prophetically, and he spoke the truth. And his audience did not want to hear it. So, what did he say?

He began his speech by proclaiming that the Western world, including the United States, had lost its courage in confronting evil. He declared that our foreign policies were based on "weakness and cowardice." And then he observed: "Should one point out that from ancient times, declining courage has been considered the beginning of the end?"[12]

Next, he attacked American democracy for its exercise of liberty without self-restraint and for its obsession with solving all problems through its legal system. His words sound like they were spoken yesterday instead of almost 40 years ago:[13]

> The defense of individual rights has reached such extremes as to make society as a whole defenseless against certain individuals . . . It is time in the West to defend not so much human rights as human obligations.
>
> Destructive and irresponsible freedom has been granted boundless space. Society appears to have little defense against the abyss of human decadence, such as, for example, the misuse of liberty for moral violence against young people [with] motion pictures full of pornography, violence and horror.

Solzhenitsyn's next target was the press. He criticized it for its lack of "moral responsibility." He declared the press to be the greatest power within the Western countries, and then he asked, "By what law has it been elected and to whom is it responsible?"[14]

He characterized the press as being full of "hastiness and superficiality," and he argued that the press has a herd mentality which gives birth "to strong mass prejudices" and "blindness."[15]

He then shifted his focus to the moral degradation of American society. He pointed to "TV stupor," "intolerable music," and "the overall decadence of art." He decried the lack of "great statesmen." And he pointed to the thin "surface film" of social stability that can easily be shattered with an electrical blackout that produces looting.[16]

He then posed the crucial question: "How did the West decline from its triumphal march to its present sickness?"[17]

He answered this question by pointing to what he called "anthropocentricity" — the elevation of Man over God, to the extent that "man [is] seen as the center of everything that exists."[18] In other words, at this point in his speech, Solzhenitsyn began to attack Humanism, the godless philosophy that has become the religion of the Western world.

He proceeded to point out that Humanism always leads to Materialism and Materialism produces "moral poverty." He made the point powerfully:[19]

> All the glorified technological achievements of Progress, including the conquest of outer space, do not redeem the 20th Century moral poverty which no one could imagine even as late as the 19th Century.

This observation brought Solzhenitsyn to his concluding and defining statement:[20]

> On the way from the Renaissance to our days, we have enriched our experience, but we

have lost the concept of a Supreme Complete
Entity which used to restrain our passions and
our irresponsibility.

We have placed too much hope in political
and social reforms, only to find out that we
were being deprived of our most precious
possession: our spiritual life. In the East, it
was destroyed by the dealings and machina-
tions of the ruling party. In the West, commercial interests suffocate it. This is the real
crisis.

It was a breathtaking, challenging and stunning presentation. It is no wonder that the negative response to it was so
strong. The wonder is that he was not lynched on the spot!

Yet, 33 years later, in 2011, the *Harvard Magazine*
published the speech in full and introduced it with these
words that must have outraged Harvard professors:[21]

Given the suffering he [Solzhenitsyn] had
endured in the Soviet Union, many in the
audience expected that the writer's address
would be a stern rebuke to Communist totali-
tarianism, combined with a paean to Western
liberty and democracy. The . . . audience was
in for a rude surprise.

"The Exhausted West," delivered in Russian with English translation under overcast
skies, chastised the arrogance and smugness
of Western materialist culture and exposed the
adverse effects of some of those achievements
that Western democracies had long prided
themselves upon . . .

Solzhenitsyn's brilliant, iconoclastic
speech ranks among the most thoughtful,

articulate and challenging addresses ever delivered at a Harvard commencement.

In like manner, Michael Novak, resident scholar at the American Enterprise Institute, has described Solzhenitsyn's Harvard speech "as the most important religious document of our time."[22]

His Greatest Speech

Solzhenitsyn in 1974.
(Wikipedia)

But Solzhenitsyn had an even more powerful and insightful speech he was yet to deliver. It came five years later in May of 1983 when he received the Templeton Prize. This is an award presented by the Templeton Foundation in Pennsylvania. It is an annual award given to a living person who, in the estimation of the judges, "has made an exceptional contribution to affirming life's spiritual dimension, whether through insight, discovery or practical works."[23]

Upon receiving the award at age 65, Solzhenitsyn delivered an address titled, "Godlessness: The First Step Toward the Gulag."[24]

He began with a reminiscence from his childhood:[25]

> More than half a century ago, while I was still a child, I recall hearing a number of older people offer the following explanation for the great disasters that had befallen Russia: *Men have forgotten God; that's why all this has happened.*

Then, picking up steam, like a black preacher who gets into a cadence and starts repeating a word or phrase, Solzhenitsyn began to emphasize his point over and over:[26]

> Since then I have spent well-nigh fifty
> years working on the history of our [Russian]
> revolution. In the process I have read hun-
> dreds of books, collected hundreds of personal
> testimonies, and have already contributed
> eight volumes of my own toward the effort to
> clear away the rubble left by that upheaval.

> But if I were asked today to formulate as
> concisely as possible the main cause of the
> ruinous revolution that swallowed up some
> sixty-million people, I could not put it more
> accurately than to repeat: *Men have forgotten
> God; that's why all this has happened.*

Nor did he leave it there. As if he wanted to make certain
that his audience was getting the point, he repeated it again:[27]

> What emerges here is a process of univer-
> sal significance. And if I were called upon to
> identify briefly the principle trait of the *entire*
> 20th Century, here too, I would be unable to
> find anything more precise and pithy to repeat
> once again: *Men have forgotten God.*

He then proceeded to warn that the Western World "is
experiencing a drying up of religious consciousness."[28] He
said this was happening because "the meaning of life in the
West has ceased to be seen as anything more than the 'pursuit
of happiness . . . .'"[29]

Another problem he identified was the refusal of people
to realize the evil that is in the individual human heart and the
consequent unwillingness to declare anything as good or evil.
The result, he declared, is that the West "is ineluctably
slipping toward the abyss."[30]

Solzhenitsyn emphasized that we in the West must come to the realization "that human salvation can be found neither in the profusion of material goods nor in merely making money." Rather, the aim should be "the quest of worthy spiritual growth." He then asserted that Mankind's hope can be found only by re-directing our consciousness "in repentance to the Creator of all; without this, no exit will be illumined, and we shall seek it in vain."[31]

Putting the same thought in different words, Solzhenitsyn concluded his remarks by urging his listeners to engage in "a determined quest for the warm hand of God, which we have so rashly and self-confidently spurned."[32]

His Concluding Years

In 1990 Solzhenitsyn's Soviet citizenship was restored, and in 1994 he and his wife returned to Russia where they settled near Moscow. He had been married twice and had fathered three sons by his second wife. He died in 2008 of heart failure at the age of 89. He was buried at a monastery in Moscow.

The Bible says that a prophet never finds honor in his own country (Mark 6:4). Nor did Solzhenitsyn in his or in his adopted country. His native country expelled him, and America shut its ears to his fervent warnings and his pleas to return to God. We are now suffering the consequences.

> *You have forgotten the God of your salvation*
> *And have not remembered the Rock of your*
> *refuge.* — Isaiah 17:10

Part 2

Current Voices

Donald Wildmon

Chapter 5

Donald Wildmon:
A Voice Crying for Decency

Let us behave properly as in the day, not in carousing and drunkenness, not in sexual promiscuity and sensuality, not in strife and jealousy. But put on the Lord Jesus Christ, and make no provision for the flesh in regard to its lusts. — Romans 13:13-14

I first became aware of Donald Wildmon's ministry — the National Federation for Decency — in 1985 when he decided to confront the huge American company called the Southland Corporation. It was the home base of more than 7,500 7-Eleven convenience stores, and Donald Wildmon became incensed when he discovered that it was the nation's largest retailer of pornographic magazines like *Playboy* and *Penthouse*.[1]

A Plea for Decency

The official sales slogan of the company at that time was, "O Thank Heaven for 7-Eleven." Wildmon thought it was ludicrous that a company with that slogan would be the number one peddler of porn. So, in 1983 he launched a public relations campaign to put pressure on the company in an effort to get them to stop selling the magazines.

The pressure continued throughout the year, and the Southland Corporation responded with silence, totally ignoring Wildmon's pleas. But a victory did occur in April of 1984 when Jack Eckerd, the founder of Eckerd Drug Stores, announced he was taking the magazines out of his 1,000 outlets.[2]

Picketing for Decency

Still, there was only silence from the Southland officials. So, in August of 1984, Wildmon called for people to form picket lines in front of 7-Eleven stores, and they did so in 168 cities. (Keep in mind this was long before you could rally people by way of the Internet.) In October, the picketing occurred again, this time at 600 stores across the nation.[3]

Southland continued to stonewall the movement — despite the fact that by the end of 1984, thousands of stores had ceased to sell the magazines (600 Super X drug stores, 400 Super America gas stations, 450 Albertsons food stores and hundreds of independently owned, franchised 7-Elevens).[4]

A March for Decency

The author and some of his staff members participated in the 1985 march against pornography.

Finally, Wildmon called for a "March Against Pornography" aimed at Southland's corporate headquarters in Dallas, Texas. It was scheduled for Labor Day, 1985. Some 13,000 concerned citizens turned out.[5] This was when I first became aware of Donald Wildmon and his ministry. My staff and I participated in that rally. We were dubbed, "evangelical terrorists" and "literary death squads" by Hugh Hefner, the publisher of *Playboy*.[6]

In April of 1986, the Southland Corporation finally capitulated and withdrew the magazines from their 4,500 corporately-owned stores. This produced a chain reaction, as 5,000 more stores pulled the magazines in the following weeks, including 2,000 Revco drug stores and 1,400 Rite Aid "family" drug stores.[7] During the ensuing months, *Playboy's* circulation dropped over 650,000 copies per month.[8]

The Man Standing for Decency

Who was this powerhouse called Don Wildmon? He had already brought Sears to its knees because his monitoring of television programs had revealed that Sears was one of the leading sponsors of trash TV — programs containing the most sex, violence and profanity. It was against this massive corporation that he launched his very first boycott in 1978. And it had been successful.[9] He was to become known as "the man the networks love to hate"[10] and "the preacher who causes heartburn in Hollywood."[11]

It seemed that a man with such enormous influence had to be a megachurch pastor or a well-known television personality. But no, before he established the National Federation for Decency in 1977, he had served for eight years as the pastor of a small United Methodist Church in Tupelo, Mississippi. During those years, it had grown from "a handful of people" to only 75 members. As Wildmon later put it, "I didn't exactly set the world on fire in those eight years."[12]

In 1976 Wildmon was moved by his bishop to a church in Southaven, Mississippi, a suburb of Memphis, Tennessee. At that point, he felt burned out. He had been an ordained minister for 20 years. He was "bored and felt constrained."

He had lost the feeling God had "something special" for him to do. Putting it more graphically, he said he "felt like a monkey in a cage, going round and round and getting nowhere."[13]

So Wildmon had no sterling record of accomplishment when God called him. But the Bible makes it clear that when God looks for a servant to anoint, outward appearances are unimportant to Him. His concern is the heart, as explained in 2 Chronicles 16:9 — "For the eyes of the LORD move to and fro throughout the earth that He may strongly support those whose heart is completely His . . ."

Don Wildmon was such a person. He was completely sold out to the Lord, and God had a plan for him that was beyond anything he could imagine.

The Decency Challenge

It all began on a December evening in 1976. His children wanted to watch TV, and when they took a look at what the three main networks had to offer, they could not find anything decent. The first program was sexually inappropriate, the second was full of foul language, and the third featured a man being beaten to death with a hammer![14]

That night, after he went to bed, Wildmon began thinking about how he could get the attention of the networks in order to impress upon them the need for wholesome programming. That's when he got an idea that would prove to be revolutionary — he would call on Christians to turn off their TV sets for a week. The next day, he drew up a press release and sent it out to all the media in Memphis. To his total shock, the Associated Press picked up his proposal, and before he could grasp what had happened, he started receiving inquiries from all across the nation.

He was 39 years old. He had no money. He had no connections with the powerful. But far more important, he had been anointed by God to take a stand for righteousness.

The "Turn the Television Off Week" was held during the week of July 24-30, 1977.[15] As soon as it was over, Wildmon resigned his pastorate, moved back to Tupelo and established his new ministry which he initially called The National Federation for Decency (the name was changed to the American Family Association in 1988). As he later put it, "I had a vision; God had a plan."[16]

A year later in 1978 his volunteers, who were monitoring television programming on the major networks, made a surprising discovery — that Sears was one of the major advertisers on programs Wildmon considered to be morally unacceptable. This led to a major crusade against Sears, and the

corporation responded positively by cutting its sponsorship of the programs.[17]

This spectacular success propelled Wildmon into the focus of the secular, hostile media. It also led to many important speaking invitations.

The Crusader Becomes a Prophet

When Wildmon first started his ministry, his only goal was to fight profanity, sex and violence on TV. But as the years passed, he realized that he was in a battle for Western Civilization and that God had called him to speak out in behalf of basic Christian values wherever they might be attacked. His response was to broaden his scope from simply a focus on television to a defense of America's Judeo-Christian consensus wherever it was assaulted by the aggressive forces of Humanism.

This broadened scope was revealed in a very important speech that he was invited to deliver to the prestigious and influential Los Angeles World Affairs Council in April of 1982. In this speech, Wildmon began speaking as a prophet, pointing to the sins of our nation and warning of their consequences.

Although his audience was a thoroughly secular one, Wildmon began by quoting Scripture:[18]

> Years ago a simple Jewish tentmaker spoke these words, "Whatsoever a man sows, that will he also reap." That truth is as valid for a nation as it is for an individual. The truth of the words of Paul of Tarsus is evident in our country today. For more than a generation now our society has been sowing seeds which are today bringing forth their fruit. Truth can be rejected, but it cannot be avoided.

He then launched into a brief review of the religious heritage of our nation, arguing that "underneath the heart of America there was always abiding a strong belief in the guiding hand of a Divine Being."[19] He then asserted, "Today, belief appears to be slowly dying, pushed aside by those whose religion is self-interest and self-indulgence."[20]

He pointed out that an "anti-religious attitude" had arisen in the nation that "no one would have dared to predict a generation ago."[21] He continued:[22]

> So strong is this anti-religious attitude that in today's atmosphere it would be impossible for Congress to make Christmas a legal holiday; to place "In God We Trust" on our coins; to include in the Pledge of Allegiance to the flag the phrase "One nation under God;" to have a chaplain open the sessions of Congress with a prayer or even to allow our armed forces to have chaplains.

At this point, Wildmon zeroed in on the fundamental problem:[23]

> Atheism and agnosticism, with their stepchildren of humanism, hedonism, and materialism, may not be the official religions of our country, but they have become the accepted practical religion by many in key positions of influence.

He continued with the observation that "any religion or philosophy which teaches us to use people and love things is a natural enemy of the Christian faith, which teaches us to love people and use things."[24]

Wildmon explained that in his opinion, "the greatest threat to the existence of our society" is "mind pollution," and the greatest instrument of such pollution is television.[25]

He asserted that his ideas were "dangerous" and have been for two thousand years. He explained that they are the ideas that resulted in Jesus being nailed to a cross and the Roman Empire killing those who held such ideas. He then presented his audience with a list of the "dangerous ideas" he was talking about:[26]

- Sex is a beautiful gift given by God to be shared between husband and wife.

- Violence is not God's way of resolving conflict.

- The elderly are an important part of society to be honored and respected for their wisdom and experience.

- Intelligent and thoughtful people can express themselves without resorting to vulgar, crude and filthy language.

- Religion is a vital part of life.

He brought this powerful and insightful presentation to a close by speaking of the inevitable consequences of abandoning our Judeo-Christian heritage:[27]

> What is at stake is whether we will remain a country accepting the Judeo-Christian concept of right and wrong, or turn our back on centuries of progress to embrace practical atheism . . .
>
> We can have a society that recognizes God and His moral standards, or we can have a society that recognizes the "make-it-up-as-you-go moral standards of Hollywood." We cannot, however, have both as equals.

He then concluded as he began, reminding his audience that "a nation which turns its back on God and His moral standards will reap what it sows . . . We are beginning to learn the party is over. It is time to pay the fiddler."[28]

The Response

Needless to say, Wildmon's comments were not well received. But that should be no surprise. Prophets are never well received — not even by believers. People have always desired "pillow prophets" who would deliver soothing words. They have despised true prophets who expose their sins and call them to repentance.

Wildmon has been viciously attacked throughout his career:

- An NBC executive branded his ministry boycotts as "the first step toward a police state."[29]

- A CBS vice president called his efforts "the greatest frontal assault on intellectual freedom this country has ever faced."[30]

- An executive with Warner Brothers studios called him a "Crypto Snake Handler."[31]

- *Playboy* magazine dubbed him "A Religious Dingbat."[32]

- The president of CBS called him "The Ayatollah of the Religious Right."[33]

- The chairman of Rite Aid drug stores characterized him as a "Rabble Rouser."[34]

- The Southern Poverty Law Center designated his ministry as a "hate group."[35]

He has been most commonly written off as a "redneck, country preacher."[36] This characterization was in response to his Southern, small town heritage and accent. But this ignores the fact that he is a man who is well educated, having earned a Bachelor's degree from Millsaps College and a Master's degree from the Chandler School of Theology.[37]

A Caricature of Wildmon.
(Supplied by the American Family Association)

A Personal Experience

I have first hand knowledge of how Wildmon has been viewed by his opponents. In 1987 he launched a protest movement against Holiday Inn because they started supplying porno movies to their rooms. I joined the protest by writing to the company to express my dismay with their new policy.

Normally, corporations respond to such messages with a carefully crafted public relations letter that is designed to put the company in the best possible light. But to my surprise, I received a personal letter from one of Holiday Inn's vice presidents, and he unloaded on me in a very emotional manner.

He said I was "obviously" one of Don Wildmon's supporters. He wondered how a person like me, "with Dr. in front of his name," could be a supporter of a "country bumpkin" like Wildmon. He concluded his letter by saying that he and all his colleagues just could not figure out how a "hick-from-the-sticks" like Wildmon could garner so much support.

I wrote back and explained it was all due to a person called the Holy Spirit.

The Worst Critics

Secular critics were not the ones that bothered Wildmon the most. Rather, what really disturbed him were the critical messages he received from pastors. He told me personally about this one time, but he also wrote rather frequently about it in his opinion column that appeared in each issue of the *AFA Journal*.

Wildmon experienced disappointment with pastors from the very beginning. When he first came up with the idea of turning off TV for a week, he thought it would be easy to get thousands involved by appealing to pastors to rally their congregations. But his appeals, even within his own denomination, were met with stony silence. This prompted him to start talking about 300,000 silent pulpits in America:[38]

> Today, 4,000 innocent precious lives of unborn babies were snuffed out . . . And 300,000 pulpits are silent . . . The networks make a mockery of Christians, the Christian faith and Christian values with nearly every show they air. Greed, materialism, violence, sexual immorality are standard fare. Program after program, movie after movie contains anti-Christian episodes and plots. News articles condescendingly refer to the "fundamentalists, right-wing Christians." Those who speak out for the sacredness of life are branded as extremists. And 300,000 pulpits are silent.

What important matters are being dealt with in our churches? The church bulletin says there will be a meeting to plan the church-wide supper. We are raising money for a new floor cover in the kitchen. (The old one doesn't match the new stove and refrigerator — we must deal with important things first.) The sermon subject last Sunday was "How To Have a Positive Attitude." And best of all — we are organizing a softball team.

Needless to say, these negative portrayals of apathetic pastors did not endear Wildmon to them. As his exposure level continued to rise in the press, many pastors began to send him critical messages.

A typical one would read: "You are just spinning your wheels. Things have gotten much worse since you started speaking out. You are not winning." Wildmon's response was one that I loved: "God didn't call me to win. He called me to stand. We will not win until Jesus returns."[39]

Regarding his secular critics and their characterization of him as a "country bumpkin," Wildmon has responded by pointing out that the reason that image has been applied to him is "because that's the way we [Christian leaders] are portrayed on television."[40]

With regard to all the criticism he has received from secular spokesmen, Wildmon has said, "I praise God for it! I consider their condemnations to be a high honor. It means I'm doing my job right."[41]

The Ministry Today

Today, the AFA Ministry operates on a budget of $20 million per year, with most of the donations averaging $20 per person. There are 400 local AFA affiliates, and the ministry has over 200 radio stations scattered throughout the nation.

They publish a monthly journal, they operate a news service, and they have recently started producing motion pictures. Over 180,000 subscribe to their journal, and they have 3.4 million subscribers to their email "Action Alerts."[42]

Pretty impressive accomplishments for a "country bumpkin"!

In 2010 Don Wildmon was forced to retire due to illness. He suffers from St. Louis Encephalitis. His son, Tim, took over the helm of the ministry.

Honors

In March of 2017, Wildmon was honored by being inducted into the National Religious Broadcasters' Hall of Fame. It is just one of many accolades he has received over the years.

One of his most significant awards was an honorary Doctor of Laws degree that was conferred on him by Asbury College in 1990. On that occasion, Dr. Dennis Kinlaw, the president of the college, made the following insightful remarks:[43]

> In the course of human history, God has shown His grace to His children in many ways. One of those ways is in His gift of prophets . . .

> Today God has looked with favor upon us and has given to our country again a prophet.

> This one came . . . from Tupelo, Mississippi . . . [and in him] we have seen again the power of one single voice, evolved by God, to touch the conscience of a nation.

> Needless to say, Don Wildmon's outspokenness has not made him popular. His

honesty and his convictions have brought him scorn, contumely, and open hostility . . .

The God of Scriptures is the God who does the unlikely. No one expected . . . a prophet of God out of Tupelo, Mississippi. But God has given us one. And today we at Asbury College give thanks.

Every time I think of Don Wildmon and his great ministry, I am reminded of the words of the Apostle Paul recorded in 1 Corinthians 1:27:

> *God has chosen the foolish things of the world to shame the wise, and God has chosen the weak things of the world to shame the things which are strong . . .*

Erwin Lutzer

Chapter 6

Erwin Lutzer:
A Voice Emphasizing
the Evil of Man

*The heart is more deceitful than all else and
is desperately sick . . .* Jeremiah 17:9

Hitler's Nightmare — could it happen here in America?
This is the question Erwin Lutzer has boldly proposed
for our nation to consider. As he points out, the answer most
people give is a resounding, "NO!"[1]

The reasons given usually include such things as:

- America's strong Christian heritage.

- Our nation's commitment to freedom
  and liberty — both in our constitution
  and in practice for over two centuries.

- The high level of education and civi-
  lized culture that characterizes our nation.

Those are good reasons, and on the surface, they seem
invincible. But they are not. Lutzer has addressed this issue
in detail, and his conclusions are chilling. In the process of
his analysis, he has spoken prophetically to our nation and
has called us to repentance lest we follow the path of Nazi
Germany.

The Man

Dr. Lutzer recording radio programs.
(Photo from The Moody Church)

Erwin Lutzer was born in 1941 in Canada and grew up on a farm near Regina, Saskatchewan. He earned a Bachelor of Theology degree from Winnipeg Bible College and then proceeded to Dallas, Texas to study at Dallas Theological Seminary where he earned a Master of Theology degree. Later he received a degree in philosophy from Loyola University in Chicago. While he was a student at Dallas Theological, he met his wife, Rebecca.[2]

In 1980 he succeeded Warren Wiersbe as Senior Pastor of The Moody Church in Chicago and served there in that capacity until 2016 when he became Pastor Emeritus. He is an award-winning author of more than twenty books, a celebrated international conference speaker, and the featured speaker on three radio programs: "The Moody Church Hour,"

"Songs in the Night," and "Running to Win." These programs are available on the Moody Broadcasting Network, the Bible Broadcasting Network, Trans World Radio and many Christian radio stations around the world.[3]

It was on May 22, 2016, after 36 years of service as Senior Pastor, that Lutzer transitioned to the role of Pastor Emeritus. In this role he acts as a "goodwill ambassador" for the Moody Church, continuing to speak, write and produce his radio programs.[4]

He and his wife, Rebecca, live in the Chicago area and are the parents of three married children. They have seven grandchildren.

Pastor Lutzer's parents were born and raised in the Ukraine in a German-speaking community. When World War I broke out in 1914, the Russian government began persecuting all people of German heritage living within its borders. His mother's parents fled to Siberia; his father's family went to Afghanistan. Both families ultimately migrated to Canada, and that's where his parents met — at church.[5]

A few years ago I was invited to be a co-speaker with Pastor Lutzer at two conferences held in the state of Illinois. I looked forward to meeting him personally, and I decided to do some research about his background. In the process I discovered that his father was 106 years old, and his mom was 100! I mentioned this when I met him, and he said it was true at the time the article was written, but that his dad had since died.

He then began chuckling to himself. I asked what was so funny. He said he was thinking about something his father told him shortly before he died. "Son," he said, "your mom and I were talking the other night about how long we have lived, and in the process, it occurred to us that most of our dear friends in Christ died 30 or more years ago. And that's when we realized that by now, they must have all come to the conclusion that when we died, we went to Hell!'"

The Concern

With regard to the example of Nazi Germany, as it applies to our nation, again, most people scoff at the idea that there could be any realistic comparison, particularly because of our strong Christian heritage. But Lutzer argues that we need to remind ourselves that pre-Nazi Germany also had a strong Christian heritage. It was, in fact, the heartland of the Reformation Movement.

Germany also contained a highly educated and erudite population, and was a land of literary giants and scientific geniuses. It was, in fact, one of the most advanced civilizations on earth.

And Germany also had a democratic government. In fact, Hitler was elected to power.

So, what happened? The German economy was destroyed by World War I and the draconian reparations the nation was required to pay after the war. Racked by a runaway inflation and widespread joblessness, the German economy created the kind of despair that will motivate people to seek desperate solutions.

Lutzer argues our nation is a sitting duck for the same type of peaceful transition to the form of totalitarian dictatorship that Hitler instituted.

Just think about it for a moment.

The Drift of Our Nation

In the 1960s we began to jettison our Christian heritage. It happened quickly and decisively, and it continues to accelerate to this day. The culture war has been won by the secularists and pagans, and we can no longer claim to be a "Christian nation." Without the inhibitions of Christian morality, the demons have been let loose. And so, on a daily basis, we witness senseless killings and gross immorality.

Churches have gotten in bed with the world, endorsing such biblical abominations as homosexuality and same-sex marriage. And they have surrendered to the demands of "tolerance" by embracing such heresies as "many roads to God." Polls show that the number of true Bible-believing Christians in America is no greater than nine percent. The Church has ceased to be a restrainer of evil.

Our level of education is certainly very high, but we have kicked God out of our educational institutions from the preschool to the graduate level. The result is a pagan education that teaches our children that there is no God and that they are simply the accidents of evolution. In short, they are being taught that they are nothing more than a higher species of animal, and they are acting like it.

Our culture is becoming increasingly depraved. Immorality is being encouraged by our government at all levels, and it is being celebrated in our movies and television programs. Hedonism and materialism are the driving forces in our culture. The dollar has become our god.

Our democratic heritage is also being rapidly undermined by the centralization of power in the national government and its ever-increasing welfare programs. More and more people are becoming wards of the state, and when it comes to voting, their only concern is which candidate will promise to give them the most "free stuff."

Our governmental leaders, particularly at the national level, have become so corrupt that we can no longer believe anything they have to say.

Our nation is becoming increasingly polarized. The two coasts are battling the center of the country. The young are fed up with having to support our exploding class of senior citizens. Blacks and Hispanics are at each other's throats.

Pagans continue to try to silence Christians.

The Needed Spark

All that is needed is a spark to set off a new civil war that will lead to the suspension of civil liberties and the institution of martial law.

Lutzer believes that spark will most likely be an over-whelming economic collapse — one far more severe than the one we experienced in 2008.[6] I also believe that because, as I said before, the dollar has become our god, and the true God of this universe is a jealous God who delights in destroying false gods.

Our economic collapse could most likely be triggered by a major terrorist attack, possibly involving nuclear weapons. Just imagine the national chaos that would occur if a nuclear device were to be detonated by a suicide crew on a merchant ship in New York harbor. It could easily happen.

The Bible makes it clear that God never pours out His wrath on a nation without warning. He will send both reme-dial judgments and prophetic voices to call a nation to repent-ance before He will deliver it to destruction.

God is doing that in America today. He responded to our Sexual Revolution in the 1960s with the Vietnam War that ended up plaguing the soul of our nation. He has sent natural disasters like Hurricane Katrina, man-made disasters like the 9/11 attacks, and economic calamities like the stock market crash of 2008.

And God has sent the prophetic voices calling the nation to repentance and warning of impending judgments.

Whereas most pastors have been reluctant to address these issues forcefully and call people to repentance, Erwin Lutzer has been speaking out strongly and fearlessly for several years, unafraid of whose toes he might step on.

As examples of what he is saying to our nation, I would point you to two sources in particular. One is a sermon of his titled, "America's Spiritual Crisis." The other is an outstanding book that was published in 2010. It is titled, *When a Nation Forgets God: 7 Lessons We Must Learn From Nazi Germany.*

A Powerful Sermon

In his sermon, Lutzer begins by going directly for the jugular, by providing a no-holds-barred definition of the problem:[7]

> Despite its foundational Christian heritage, America is rapidly degenerating into a godless society. The Church in America, although highly visible and active, appears powerless to redirect the rushing secular currents. Mired in moral and spiritual crisis, America's only hope is a national revival, like God has graciously bestowed in the past.

He proceeds to emphasize the way in which our leaders are doing everything they can to erase God from America's consciousness.[8]

> The powers in America today . . . have chosen a path of rejecting God and His ways. Federal courts have interpreted our constitution as requiring that the Bible, prayer and religious discussion be removed from classrooms, community buildings and places of public gatherings. Government officials and educators across the country are systematically eliminating any vestiges of God from society. Militant secularists will not be satisfied until God is expunged from every fact of American life.

As for Christianity in particular, Lutzer declares that "society is becoming openly hostile to Christian values."[9] In this regard, he points out that "the media trivializes and ridicules Christianity in the name of humanistic and pluralistic concerns."[10] Commenting further on the influence of the media, he sounds like an echo of Donald Wildmon:[11]

> American culture is dominated by television and movies, whose profanity and lewdness tramp God's honor into the mud, inculcating non-Christian values from infancy. Public schools teach our children how to practice various forms of immorality. One school curriculum in America teaches acceptance of homosexuality in the first grade and mutual masturbation in junior high . . . America is reaping the dire consequences of rejecting God. Our society is morally bankrupt, and the problems seem resistant to government cures.

As a pastor, Lutzer is particularly concerned about the waning influence of the Church. He declares:[12]

> The Church in America, despite its many activities and apparent successfulness, has had no measurable affect in reversing the downward spiral . . . Sadly, the influence has been in the wrong direction, as we see evidence that our culture has begun to permeate our churches. The Church is seduced by the social agenda of wealth and pleasure, and has condoned sinful compromises.

An Insightful Book

In Lutzer's book, *When A Nation Forgets God*, he begins by asserting that "Yes, Nazi Germany has some lessons to teach us."[13] Following up on that observation, he writes:[14]

I am aware, of course that parallels between Nazi Germany and the United States can easily be overdrawn, but this danger should not stop us from learning some hard lessons from that dark period when the Church struggled to find its identity and had to suffer for what it believed . . . those similarities are happening before our eyes.

Nazism did not arise in a vacuum. There were cultural streams that made it possible . . Some of those streams — myths accepted by the masses — are in evidence in America today, and hence this book . . .

There were circumstances and widely accepted ideas that enabled the population to become a part of an evil that was greater than that of any individual. The gas ovens were the end result of certain political and religious trends that made the horrors possible.

Lutzer then illustrates his point with a quote from the writings of Viktor Frankl (1905-1997), the famous psychoanalyst who was a Holocaust survivor:[15]

The gas chambers of Auschwitz were the ultimate consequence of the theory that man is nothing but the product of heredity and environment — or as the Nazis liked to say, "of blood and soil."

Focusing once again on American society, Lutzer observes:[16]

Today we face cultural pressures that are forcing us to combine Christ with other religions, or to combine Christ with a political or ideological agenda. The experience of the Church in Nazi Germany reminds us that

> Christ must always stand alone; He must be worshiped not as One who stands alongside the governmental leaders of this world, but as standing above them as *King of kings and Lord of lords*.
>
> Whether it's Nazism, Marxism or Secularism, the state is always in conflict with religious freedom.

Following this disturbing introduction, Lutzer launches into the heart of his book by outlining seven lessons he believes Americans need to learn from Nazi Germany. The seven are listed below, with a quote from each section.

1) **When God is separated from government, judgment follows.**[17]

"And so it was that secularism was imposed

on the German people. The role of the Church was minimized by privatizing faith and instituting laws about what could or could not be said from a pulpit."[18]

2) It's always the economy.[19]

"When given a choice, most people probably will choose bread and sausage above the free market and individual liberties."[20]

3) That which is legal might also be evil.[21]

"When God is separated from government, we are forced to accept arbitrary laws. Either God is the lawgiver or Man is; either we derive our laws from theistic universal values, or we say that the individual countries or cultures are the lawgivers. Either God is supreme or the state is supreme . . . a court can make abortion legal, but it cannot make it moral . . . *Show me your laws and I will show you your God.*"[22]

4) Propaganda can change a nation.[23]

"Perhaps the most enduring lesson of Nazi Germany is that ordinary people, simply concerned about living their own lives, can be motivated to become a part of an evil movement through the power of compelling propaganda, intimidation and mass euphoria."[24]

5) Parents — not the state — are responsible for a child's training.[25]

"Today's law in Germany that makes home schooling illegal reminds us of a Nazi-era law instigated by Hitler back in 1938. He declared that public education was compulsory and that children could not be educated in the home.

The state, not the family or the Church had first dibs regarding the child's education."[26]

6) Ordinary heroes can make a difference.[27]

"'When God calls a man, He bids him come and die,' wrote Dietrich Bonhoeffer during the dark days when the Church in Germany was being Nazified. And at the age of 39, he practiced what he preached; he was hanged on the gallows and died . . . Today in America we need an army of ordinary heroes to stand against the gathering darkness in our land. We need people who will stand for truth courageously, consistently, and with humility and grace."[28]

7) We must exalt the Cross in the gathering darkness.[29]

". . . without the Cross we pound a nail in our coffin! There is a danger that we become so overburdened with social/political agendas that our message is lost amid our many cultural skirmishes. The Church has always faced the temptation to modify the Gospel or make it secondary to a given political, philosophical or cultural agenda . . . God is neither Republican nor Democrat. When the Cross is wrapped in the flag of a political party, it is always distorted or diminished."[30]

In conclusion, Lutzer points out how we as Christians have allowed the culture to divert our eyes from Jesus onto ourselves:[31]

In the evangelical community, psychology is substituted for theology and cheap grace has replaced what Bonhoeffer described as "costly grace." In short, we have lost our intellectual and spiritual center and replaced it with consumerism, self-help and the quest for personal advantage. We are self-absorbed rather than God-absorbed. And we can see the results.

Concluding Thoughts

We need to keep in mind that the potential for the evil of Hitler resides in all of us. The Bible states that "the heart is more deceitful than all else and is desperately sick" (Jeremiah 17:9). Jesus affirmed this when He asserted that all evil — both thoughts and actions — come out of the heart (Matthew 15:19-20 and Mark 7:20-23). Over and over the Bible asserts that the nature of Man is evil and should never be trusted:

Psalm 53:1-3

1) The fool has said in his heart, "There is no God," they are corrupt, and have committed abominable injustice; there is no one who does good.

2) God has looked down from heaven upon the sons of men to see if there is anyone who understands, who seeks after God.

3) Every one of them has turned aside; together they have become corrupt; there is no one who does good, not even one.

Psalm 118:8-9

8) It is better to take refuge in the LORD than to trust in man.

9) It is better to take refuge in the LORD than to trust in princes.

This fundamental truth about the nature of Man was reflected in the most surprising quotation I ran across while doing research on Lutzer's writings. I found the quote in the writings of Charlie Chaplin's son, Charles Jr. He says that in 1940 while his father was filming his parody of Hitler, *The Great Dictator*, he was "haunted" by the similar backgrounds of Hitler and himself. He explains:[32]

> Their desires were poles apart. One was to make millions weep, while the other was to set the whole world laughing. Dad could never think of Hitler without a shudder, half of horror, half of fascination. "Just think," he would say uneasily, "he's the madman. I'm the comic. But it could have been the other way around."

That profound insight is true of all of us. We are born with a fallen sin nature. We have to learn the difference between good and evil. That knowledge comes from God's Word, and we learn it either from our parents or from the Church, or both. When God is ejected from society and the Church is either marginalized or suppressed, evil is let loose, and "God gives the society over to a depraved mind" (Romans 1:28). That's where we are in America today.

We are literally begging for the fate of ancient Judah when that nation turned against God and refused to repent, despite the infliction of many remedial judgments and the warnings of prophets.

Erwin Lutzer's message can be summed up in one sentence — *America, stop trusting in men and place your trust instead in God.*

David Jeremiah

Chapter 7

David Jeremiah:
A Voice Decrying Rebellion

For rebellion is as the sin of divination, And insubordination is as iniquity and idolatry. Because you have rejected the word of the LORD, He has also rejected you . . .
1 Samuel 15:23

One does not normally think of a pastor as being a prophet. Pastors speak soothing words about God's love. Prophets thunder about sin and God's wrath. Pastors seem to have supernatural patience. Prophets are impulsive and demanding. People love pastors. Prophets are tolerated, at best.

Back in the 1980s when I held 40 to 45 meetings a year, starting on Sunday morning and going through Wednesday evening, people would come up to me and say, "Why doesn't our pastor ever preach with your bluntness and passion?" My response always was: "If he did, you would run him off within a year's time, if not sooner!"

A pastor has to be willing to preach his heart out Sunday after Sunday and see almost no visible change in his congregation — and yet continue to love them anyway. The prophet, on the other hand, wants to grab people by the shoulders and shake them until their teeth rattle, demanding that they stop playing church and start living for Jesus.

Pastor Prophets

That's why I find it so interesting that so many of the most forceful prophetic voices in America today are pastors — like Erwin Lutzer, Jonathan Cahn, Robert Jeffress and David Jeremiah. Equally interesting is that very few true prophetic voices are found among those who have committed their lives to the teaching and preaching of Bible prophecy. They seem more concerned about arguing over the timing of the Rapture or the sequence of end time events than speaking prophetically to the Church and the nation about the reality of sin, the need for repentance, and the danger of impending judgment.

David Jeremiah has said of himself that his calling in life was neither to be an author nor a prophet. Rather, he describes himself as a "pastor-teacher."[1] But he readily admits that due to the rapid deterioration of society in recent years and the threat it presents to religious freedom, he has reluctantly taken on the role of speaking and writing prophetically.[2] As he puts it, "I cannot sit idly by and watch believers be 'destroyed for a lack of knowledge'"[3] (Hosea 4:6).

And when it comes to speaking as a prophet, David Jeremiah has few equals. Consider his characterization of the current American social scene:[4]

America is rolling in luxury, reveling in excesses, rollicking in pleasure, reeling in drunkenness, revolting in morals, and rotting in sin. America has rejected the God of its youth and has raised up in His place the idols made with its own hands. We have programmed God out of our schools, our government, our homes, and even our churches . . .

America is out of tune. The nation has lost its pitch by removing God from its life, thus producing the dissonant chords of cynicism

and apathy. Into this cacophony of hopeless-
ness, God calls His people to sound a clear A
so the world can hear above the discord the
heavenly note of hope.

The Pastor Turned Prophet

Who is this pastor-teacher turned prophet with the last
name of one of the greatest of the Hebrew prophets?

David Paul Jeremiah was born in 1941 in Toledo, Ohio.
At the age of 11, his parents moved to Akron, Ohio where his
father, James, who was a Baptist pastor, took over as president of Cedarville College, a Baptist institution (which assumed university status in 2002).[5]

David followed in his father's footsteps. He graduated
from Cedarville College in 1963. That same year he married
his college sweetheart, Donna. They moved to Dallas, Texas
where David attended Dallas Theological Seminary.

In 1981 he and his family moved to El Cajon, California
where he took over Scott Memorial Baptist Church which had
been pastored for 25 years by Tim LaHaye. The church's
name was later changed to Shadow Mountain Community
Church.

David Jeremiah

Today that church averages an attendance of over 10,000
each Sunday. Jeremiah has a radio program called Turning
Point that is broadcast worldwide. The television version
went nationwide in the year 2000. Jeremiah is also a writer,

having authored more than 50 books.

He and his wife, Donna, have four children and 12 grand-children.

His Prophetic Message

David Jeremiah speaks about America with a broken heart. His utter dismay over the disintegration of our nation is reflected in the title of his most important prophetic book: *I Never Thought I'd See The Day!* (2011). He sums up his feeling with these words: "When I look at the changes that have occurred in the land I love — and the Church I love even more — just in my lifetime, I have to pinch myself to see if it's a dream gone bad. Sadly, what I see is all too real."[6]

He puts much of the blame on the Church for the drift of America into secularism. Regarding Christians, he says the truth is that "we can echo the words of Pogo in the old Walt Kelly comic strip: 'We have met the enemy and he is us!'"[7] This is demonstrated in the fact that the lifestyles of most Christians can no longer be distinguished from the lifestyles of the world because "we have allowed the world to *conform* us to its image instead of allowing the Holy Spirit and the Word of God to *transform* us into the image of Christ" (Romans 8:29).[8]

Jeremiah addresses "nine developments that I never thought I would see in my lifetime:"[9]

1) The rise of angry atheists.

2) The intensifying of spiritual warfare.

3) The dethroning of Jesus Christ.

4) The redefining of marriage.

5) The loss of our moral compass.

6) The marginalization of the Bible.

7) The growing irrelevance of the Church.

8) The growing influence of rogue nations.

9) The erosion of America's support for Israel.

Jeremiah devotes a chapter to each one of these destructive developments, and along the way, he provides many insights:

- "Atheists claim to believe that God does not exist, and yet, according to empirical studies [they] tend to be the people most angry at Him."[10]

- ". . . a large number of pastors and teachers ignore or downplay spiritual warfare to the point that many professing Christians don't even know they're at war."[11]

- "Jesus is no longer given most-favored-religious-leader status . . ."[12]

- "Cohabitation without marriage has become so common that in a mere thirty years it has effected a complete inversion of America's attitude toward a practice that the Bible unambiguously labels *sin*."[13]

- "Our [nation's] moral compass seems no longer to have a 'true north' . . . It's as if immorality is in the water we drink and the air we breathe."[14]

- "As much as I hate to say it, the public square and public schools are not the only venues in which the Bible's status has been downplayed and its meaning diluted. It's also happening in the last place we should expect it: in the Christian Church itself."[15]

- "Unfortunately, biblical Christianity is no longer being preached from every pulpit in the land. As a result, America is losing her spiritual way, and it is due, in no small part, to the fact that the Church has lost *her* way. I believe with all my heart: As goes the Church, so goes the nation."[16]

- "I believe America's future depends in large part on one simple factor: our relationship to the tiny nation of Israel. And given the political trends in recent years, I believe America is putting her future at risk."[17]

- ". . . as I read my Bible, I find compelling reasons to believe that the human race is on a collision course with calamity — that things are going to get worse before they get better, which will not happen until the return of Jesus Christ to earth. I believe the Bible teaches that in the last days of this age, only the return of Christ will keep humanity from destroying itself."[18]

The Sequel

In 2016, five years after the publication of *I Thought I Would Never See the Day!*, Jeremiah published a sequel entitled, *Is This the End?* The subtitle was, "Signs of God's Providence in a Disturbing New World."

He begins this book by looking back at the 5 year interval, and he expresses dismay over the continuing and accelerating disintegration of the Judeo-Christian foundation of our nation. He laments that "those cracks that riddled America's foundation have spread into gaping fissures, and many more have appeared."[19] He declares that morality in our nation "is no longer in free fall; it has hit bottom."[20]

He proceeds to paint a dark verbal picture of our nation's spiritual condition:[21]

> In today's America, anything goes. Christianity is no longer merely pushed aside; American Christians are now experiencing overt repression and even persecution. Civility in politics has disappeared. Corruption and dishonesty in government is rampant and open. Race relations are deteriorating, earnings are declining, civic disorder is accelerating, and the national debt is beyond control.

In trying to understand why all this has happened to our nation, Jeremiah proposes two explanations, one historical and the other biblical.

He asserts that the historical basis is rooted in the philosophy of Humanism which he describes as "The unifying belief . . . [that] God, if he exists, is irrelevant. Humanity is calling the shots, and humans are evolving biologically, socially, governmentally, and morally."[22] He sums up the meaning of this philosophy with these words: "Forget about answering to a Holy Creator. We are responsible for ourselves."[23]

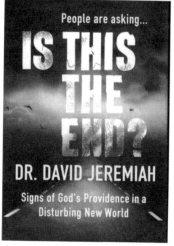

The biblical way of understanding the destruction of our national morality is to be "found in humanity's rebellion against the holy character of God as explained in His Word."[24] And the "bottom-line reason" for this rebellion is because we desire to live as we please, without being accountable to anyone. Therefore, a Creator God is unthinkable, and so "our society has chosen to believe the unbelievable — that everything came from nothing in an unexplainable explosion of dense matter with an inexplicable origin . . ."[25]

Jeremiah reminds us that when the ancient nation of Judah reached the same stage of rebellion that we are in, "the holy God could no longer live with a nation that had descended into depravity," and so His Shekinah Glory departed the Jewish Temple (Ezekiel 10 and 11). In effect, God stamped the word, "Ichabod," on the nation, meaning "The glory has departed."[26]

Christian Persecution

Jeremiah stresses the growth of intolerance in our nation toward Christianity as expressed in the suppression of Christian speech and actions. "Christianity is being pushed to the edges," he declares, "because its adherence to biblical morality is at odds with the philosophy of unrestrained freedom that now dominates America's cultural landscape."[27]

This growing intolerance is increasingly being expressed in out-right persecution of Christians. He identifies five stages of that persecution as follows:[28]

1) Stereotyping[29]
   The characterization of Christians in movies and TV programs as "ignorant, uneducated, backward, inhibited, homophobic, hateful and intolerant."

2) Marginalizing[30]
   Pushing the Church out of the public arena by arguing that Christians have freedom of religion only in the sense that they can do what they please within the confines of their church buildings.

3) Threatening[31]

Making it clear that any exercise of one's Christian convictions in the public arena will result in disciplinary action, mandatory sensitivity training or even the loss of a job.

4) Intimidating[32]

Personal harassment and ridicule of those with Christian morals.

5) Litigating[33]

Taking Christians to court to force compliance with laws that violate their consciences and making them pay fines or even serve time in prison.

A Surprising Interjection

Despite the despairing picture that Jeremiah presents about our nation, he gives a surprising answer to a crucial question he asks himself.

The question: "Is there hope?"[34]

The answer: "I can answer with an unqualified and resounding yes!"[35]

He explains his answer by stating that the key to all our nation's problems is spiritual revival, and he believes that revival is possible.[36]

I think it is interesting that Erwin Lutzer has taken the same position and for the same reason.[37] Both men argue that our God is a God of Hope, that with Him all things are possible, and that American history proves that revival can happen when there seems little hope for it.

The latter point is particularly stressed by both pastors. They point to the great revivals or "awakenings" that occurred in this nation in the early 1700s and 1800s, in the mid-

1800s, in the early 1900s, and even in the 1970s.[38]

In each case they point out that our nation had grown cold in the Lord. True believers prayed earnestly for revival, and God responded by sending it.

I cannot help but think that in expressing this hope for revival, both Lutzer and Jeremiah are speaking from pastor's hearts, with the resolve that they must provide people with hope, even if it is an unreal one.

And I personally believe the ardent hope for revival is unreal. It is one thing to grow cold in the Lord. It is an entirely different thing to become hot in rebellion against the Lord. And that is precisely where we are as a nation. Collectively, we are shaking our fist at God and telling Him in no uncertain terms, "We will do as we damn well please!"

We have even resorted to openly mocking God and His Word. Take for example the proclamations our presidents have been issuing each June to celebrate and honor the Moral Perversion Movement of LGBTQ (Lesbian, Gay, Bisexual, Transgender, and Questioning). Or consider the blatantly blasphemous way in which President Obama lit up the White House with the rainbow colors of the LGBTQ Movement in celebration of our Supreme Court's legalization of same-sex marriage.

We are a nation in open rebellion against God and His Word, and as such, we are a nation literally begging for God's judgment.

And the nail in the coffin has been the way we have turned our back on Israel, refusing to recognize the historically proven truth that those who curse Israel will be cursed, just as those who bless Israel will be blessed (Genesis 12:3).

A Biblical Example

Both Lutzer and Jeremiah have also pointed to biblical

examples of unexpected revival — the most significant being the revival that took place in Judah following the reign of 55 long years by its most evil sovereign, King Manasseh (2 Chronicles 33).[39] It is true that a remarkable revival occurred when Manasseh was succeeded by a righteous young king named Josiah who gave his heart to the Lord and set about to purify the Jewish Temple and resurrect the people's knowledge of God's Word.

But 31 years later when Josiah was killed on the battlefield, the nation of Judah quickly reverted to its sinful ways, and God poured out His wrath on the nation by destroying it through the Babylonians. The problem was that evil had become intertwined in the fabric of the nation, and it was awaiting under the veneer of revival to assert itself with gusto.

This biblical example is really not applicable to our nation's situation. We are a representative democracy. Ancient Judah was ruled by a monarchy, and the king could impose his reforms from the top, creating a veneer of revival that really did not encompass the population.

Yes, we have been granted a momentary reprieve from our headlong rush into debauchery through the unexpected election of Donald Trump. But he is no Josiah. Nor is he even a choir boy. He has a despicable personal background. He is a pragmatist with no strong values. Even worse, he is an egomaniacal person who believes he can "make America great again." The only person who can do that is Jesus, and we have turned our back on Him.

To his credit, Jeremiah realizes politics is not the answer to our nation's rebellion against God:[40]

> America cannot be saved by politics. It is
> not going to be saved by Republicans, Demo-
> crats or Independents. While we need wise
> and godly national leaders, the real answer to

our problems is not political but spiritual. We are not going to be saved by our economists or educators. The answer is not found in being liberal or conservative, but in being committed to Jesus Christ.

Conclusion

Yes, our God is a God of Hope (Romans 15:13). But there are limits to His patience. Yes, with Him, all things are possible, but the Bible clearly reveals how He deals with a rebellious nation which He has blessed. And part of His pattern is to designate a point of no return, when His remedial judgments will give way to destruction.

In the last chapter of this book, I will show you in the Scriptures where the threshold of no return exists and why I believe we have already crossed it.

So, is there any hope? Even when there is no hope for a society, there is always hope for individuals within that society who have placed their faith in Jesus as their Lord and Savior. And part of that hope is the Rapture of the Church — a glorious promise of God that David Jeremiah strongly emphasizes.[41]

And he places the timing of that event before the beginning of the Tribulation for many reasons. One in particular just jumps off the page:

> . . . in all the New Testament, there is not one single statement to warn Christians of the coming Great Tribulation or to help them prepare for it. If it were our lot to endure the wrath that will devastate the earth during those seven years, isn't it strange that God never gave us one tidbit of information, encouragement, warning, or instruction on our preparation for it? The reason for that omission is

clear: the church will not be present at all
when the Tribulation comes.

In fact, the book of Revelation contains a promise that
true believers will be exempted from the Tribulation: "Because you have kept the word of My perseverance, I also will
keep you from the hour of testing, that hour which is about to
come upon the whole world, to test those who dwell on the
earth" (Revelation 3:10).

Now folks, that is what I call hope — genuine hope,
because it is an iron-clad promise from the God of Hope.

William Koenig

Chapter 8

William Koenig:
A Voice of Warning
Concerning Israel

For behold, in those days and at that time,
when I restore the fortunes of Judah and
Jerusalem, I will gather all the nations and
bring them down to the valley of Jehoshaphat.
Then I will enter into judgment with them
there on behalf of My people and My inheri-
tance, Israel, whom they have scattered
among the nations; and they have divided up
My land. — Joel 3:1-2

The call God has placed on William Koenig's life is every bit as unusual as that of Don Wildmon. No one would ever have guessed that either one of them would end up serving as powerful prophetic voices for the Lord.

Bill Koenig was a hard-driving commercial real estate developer in Dallas, Texas when he encountered the Lord Jesus Christ. Christianity was something that was not un-known to him — he just didn't know Jesus. He had grown up in a small Arizona town located south of Phoenix. He had attended the Episcopal Church most Sundays with his mom and brother. He believed in God and had served as an altar boy, but he had no personal relationship with Jesus. He was a classic cultural Christian.[1]

Koenig graduated from Arizona State University with a degree in communications. He embarked on a real estate career which led him to the Dallas, Texas area in 1979. Five years later, he decided to start his on brokerage and investment company.

A Transforming Breakfast

One day two of his commercial real estate colleagues invited him to a weekly breakfast meeting sponsored by a ministry called Priority Living. On the way back from the meeting, Koenig asked one of his hosts, "Where did the speaker get the information he shared with us? Were those his ideas?" His host responded, "He got them from the Bible."[2]

From that point on, Koenig says he "couldn't read enough of the Bible and Christian books." He tried to make up for lost time by attending as many Christian conferences and meetings as he could. In the Fall of 1988, he surrendered his life to Jesus as his Lord and Savior.[3] He had no idea what an unusual future the Lord had in store for him.

Discovering God's Love for Israel

As Koenig started digging into the Scriptures, the Lord began to speak to his heart about how much He loved the Jewish people and what a glorious future He has planned for them. That's when Koenig realized that the Replacement Theology being taught by the Catholic Church and the majority of Protestant denominations was completely unbiblical. This is the theology that teaches that God has washed His hands of the Jewish people and has replaced them with the Church, transferring all the blessings to the Church that He had promised Israel.

Koenig was also impressed with the many prophecies God is fulfilling among the Jewish people today — such as their regathering from all over the world back to their homeland and the consequent re-establishment of their state.

Additionally, he was deeply troubled by the anti-Semitism that he witnessed in press reports about Israel that were written by journalists all over the world. It was clear to him that a double standard of conduct was being applied to Israel. The press seemed always to take the position that Israel could do no good and the Arabs could do no wrong.

A Major Career Change

These concerns continued to mount until Koenig reached the point where he could no longer contain them. During the summer of 1996 he began writing a weekly summary of Middle East news from a biblical perspective, and he also began speaking out against Replacement Theology. He placed his articles on the Internet and called his endeavor, "Koenig International News."[4]

The word about his insightful articles spread fast, and before long, Koenig felt called to give up his real estate and financial career in order to devote himself full time to his unique news ministry. In 2001 he and his wife, Claudia, decided to move to Washington, D.C. where he could get his fingers on the pulse of the news first hand. Amazingly, in short order he was certified as a White House correspondent.[5]

Today, he continues to write a weekly news report called "Koenig's Eye View from the White House." It is posted on his website called "World Watch Daily" (watch.org). His news service has readers and email sub-

Koenig in the White House Rose Garden.

scribers in all 50 U.S. states and 105 countries.[6]

In 2004 Koenig's outreach seemed to take on a prophetic mantle when he published an extraordinary book titled, *Eye to Eye: Facing the Consequences of Dividing Israel.*[7]

Early Warnings

Actually, Koenig had been speaking prophetically before this book was published. He had already emerged as one of Christendom's foremost critics of Replacement Theology, and he had repeatedly warned that the efforts of our government to force Israel to surrender the heart of its homeland (Judea and Samaria) would result in judgments of God upon our nation in accordance with Genesis 12:3 which says that God will curse those who curse the Jewish people.

He related the wide-spread acceptance of Replacement Theology to the ignorance of Bible prophecy:[8]

> Today there are approximately 100 million American church members who have very little to no understanding of Bible prophecy. These church members are from Replacement Theology churches that don't teach Bible prophecy and who look at prophetic scriptures as allegorical and not literal. Consequently, they do not understand the importance of Israel to the God of Israel or God's redemptive plan for Israel and the nations . .

> So, the prophecies in Scripture concerning the blessing and restoration of Israel to the Promised Land are "spiritualized" or "allegorized" into promises of God's blessing for the Church . . .

Koenig then makes a very keen observation about the history of the Jewish people:[9]

If Israel has been condemned by God [as Replacement Theology claims], and there is no future for the Jewish nation, how do we explain the supernatural survival of the Jewish people over the past 2,000 years despite the many attempts to destroy them? How do we explain why and how Israel reappeared as a nation in the 20th Century after not existing for 1,900 years?

A Seminal Book

The thesis of Koenig's 2004 book, *Eye to Eye*, was that many of the natural calamities, economic setbacks and political crises experienced by the United States since 1991 were directly related to actions taken by our government to force Israel to surrender territory to the Arabs.

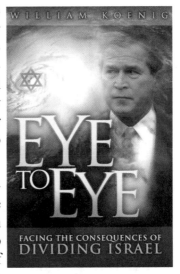

He selected 1991 as his starting point because that was the year that the Bush Administration (George H. W.) forced Israel to begin the appeasement process of "trading land for peace." He viewed this arm-twisting as the turning point in US-Israel relations. Koenig often points out that Zechariah 12:1-3 says that in the end times all the nations of the world will come against Israel over the issue of the control of Jerusalem. He views 1991 as the year when we joined the other nations of the world in pressuring the Israelis to give up their heartland of Judea and Samaria (which the world calls "The West Bank") and to surrender their sovereignty over east Jerusalem.

The book had a very prophetic cover. It showed President George W. Bush looking over his right shoulder directly into the eye of a hurricane, over which was superimposed a Star of David. Keep in mind that this was one year before Hurricane Katrina which occurred while the Bush Administration was forcing Israel to abandon the Gaza Strip.

The title of the book, *Eye to Eye*, was suggested by Koenig's wife. She took it from Matthew Henry's commentary on Isaiah 52:8 where he wrote: "They [the watchmen] shall see an exact agreement and correspondence between the prophecy and the events, the promise and the performance; they shall see how they look upon another *eye to eye*, and be satisfied that the same God spoke the one and did the other."[10] In other words, in the end times there will be people who are prophetically gifted to recognize the correspondence between Bible prophecies and world events.

Supernatural Correlations

In his book Koenig shows the amazing parallels between U.S. mistreatment of Israel and subsequent natural calamities, economic setbacks and political crises. In the original edition, he listed a total of 53 catastrophes in the 13 years between 1991 and 2004 that were related to our mistreatment of Israel. Here are just a few of those examples:

The Madrid Conference[11] — This conference, which we forced on Israel, marked the beginning of the "land for peace" process. The opening of the conference on October 30, 1991, coincided with the formation of "the Perfect Storm." This was the record breaking storm along our Atlantic seacoast which produced 100 foot high waves and heavily damaged President Bush's home at Kennebunkport, Maine. The headlines of *USA Today* on November 1, 1991, had the stories of the storm and the Madrid Conference side by side.

Round Six of the Bilateral Peace Talks[12] — In June of 1992 Yitzhak Rabin was elected the new Prime Minister of Israel.

We immediately insisted that he come to Washington, D.C. and meet with Yasser Arafat. The day that meeting began, August 24, 1992, Hurricane Andrew slammed into Florida with winds of 177 miles per hour. The damage done amounted to over $30 billion — the most costly hurricane in U.S. History to that point in time.

The Camp David Summit[13] — From July 11 through July 24 in the summer of 2000, President Clinton hosted a summit conference between Israel and the Palestinian Authority. Clinton pressured Israeli Prime Minister Ehud Barak to surrender the heartland of Israel. During these precise dates, a major heat wave struck the South Central U.S. and fires broke out in our Western states. At one point, there were over 50 active fires that consumed over 500,000 acres before the end of the month.

U.S.-Saudi Plan to Divide Israel[14] — According to the *Washington Post*, for the 17 days prior to the 9/11 terrorist attacks on the World Trade Center and the Pentagon, the Bush Administration had been negotiating with the Saudi Arabians to develop a comprehensive plan for dividing Israel. Most of the work had been completed by September 10, with the purpose of having the U.S. Secretary of State present the plan to the United Nations on September 24. On September 11 the deadliest attack ever to occur on American soil took place, resulting in the deaths of almost 3,000 people — more Americans than died in the Pearl Harbor attack in 1941 or the D-Day invasion in 1944.

White House Ramadan Celebration[15] — On Thursday evening, November 7, 2002, President Bush hosted a dinner at the White House to honor the Muslim religious holiday called Ramadan. In his speech that evening, the President said:

> . . . this season commemorates the revelation
> of God's word in the holy Koran to the pro-
> phet Muhammad. Today this word inspires

faithful Muslims to lead lives of honesty and
integrity and compassion . . . We see in Islam
a religion that traces its origins back to God's
call on Abraham . . .

Two days later a total of 88 tornados hit Arkansas, Tennessee, Alabama, Mississippi, Georgia, Ohio, and Pennsylvania.

The Middle East Peace Plan[16] — On April 30, 2003, U.S.
Ambassador Daniel Kurtzer presented the "Road Map" peace
plan to Israeli Prime Minister Ariel Sharon. It was a plan
formulated by an ungodly coalition called "the Quartet." This
group was made up of Russia, the European Union, the
United Nations, and the United States. It called for Israel to
surrender Gaza and its heartland of Judea and Samaria to the
Palestinians. On May 4th Secretary of State Colin Powell met
with terrorist leader Hafez al-Assad of Syria and made a commitment to him to include the surrender of the Golan Heights
in the peace plan. That day a swarm of tornados began tearing
apart the Central United States. Over the next 7 days, there
was a total of 412 tornados — the largest cluster ever observed by NOAA since it began its record keeping in 1950.
The previous record had been 177 in 1999.

In summary, between October 1991 and November 2004,
the United States experienced:[17]

- 9 of the 10 largest insurance events in U.S. history.

- 9 of the 10 greatest natural disasters as ranked by
  FEMA relief costs.

- 5 of the costliest hurricanes in U.S. history.

- 3 of the 4 largest tornado swarms in U.S. history.

All of which were linked to our attempts to pressure Israel
into either dividing up its land or surrendering part of its
capital city of Jerusalem.

The world would laugh and call these coincidences, but I don't believe in coincidence. I believe only in God-incidences. God is sovereign. He is in control.

The Gaza Withdrawal

In the 2008 revision of his book, Koenig expanded his examples of God's remedial judgments to include the year of 2005. Particularly interesting is what he had to say about Hurricane Katrina.[18]

He pointed out that the most recent tragic event in Israel was the forced withdrawal of all Jews from Gaza. It began on August 7, 2005 and continued through the 22nd, as nearly 9,000 Israelis were uprooted from their land and homes. Many had been in the area for as long as 35 years.

It was a heart-wrenching event to watch women and children manhandled, synagogues violated, torah scrolls desecrated, houses bulldozed, graves dug up, and farms destroyed. Entire Jewish communities were forcibly removed from land which God has given to the Jewish people as an everlasting possession (Psalm 105:8-11).

The economic impact on the Israeli economy was significant. The farms in Gaza represented 70% of Israel's organic produce, 60% of the nation's exported herbs, 15% of its total agricultural exports, 60% of its exported cherry tomato crop, and $120 million of its flower exports.

And while this travesty was taking place, Secretary of State Condoleezza Rice began applying more pressure with the following statement: "Everyone empathizes with what the Israelis are facing . . . but it cannot be Gaza only."[19]

The Supernatural Response

The withdrawal ended on August 22nd, and on the very next day, the government of Bermuda announced that a tropical depression had formed off its coast. Dubbed "Katrina," the storm quickly developed into the most powerful hurricane in modern history. It slammed into New Orleans and the Mississippi coast four days later on the 27th. The hurricane disrupted 25% of our crude oil production and destroyed our nation's largest port (the 5th largest in the world in terms of tonnage).

The hurricane hit just three days before New Orleans — which often refers to itself proudly as "Sin City USA" — was scheduled to host an ungodly event that had come to be called "The Gay Mardi Gras." The theme that year was to be "Jazz and Jezebels." The previous year the event had drawn 125,000 revelers who proudly flaunted their perversion publicly in a parade that featured the bizarre. Incredibly, this event is sponsored by a group that has named itself "Southern Decadence."

The consequences of the storm were national in scope. It resulted in higher fuel prices which led to higher prices for all goods. It disrupted the flow of goods into and out of our country. It resulted in a significant increase in our national debt. It shamed us before the world as we mishandled the aftermath. And it deeply scarred the Bush Administration.

The Truth of Remedial Judgments

Koenig's characterization of these calamities as remedial judgments of God did not sit well with many Christian spokesmen — particularly the liberal leaders who scoff at Bible prophecy, reject the supernatural and argue that the Church has replaced Israel. They tended to look on his analysis as superstitious nonsense.

But I would strongly contend that Koenig is right on target. The Bible reveals that God has always used remedial judgments to call nations to repentance, and those judgments have often consisted of national calamities. Further, the Bible teaches that God does not change (Malachi 3:6). He is the same yesterday, today and tomorrow (Hebrews 13:8).

What God did in Bible times, He can do today. But we have been brainwashed by Western scientific rationalism into rejecting the supernatural. Science says that for something to exist, you must be able to see it, measure it, weigh it or dissect it.

In contrast, the Bible teaches there is a whole realm of the supernatural that cannot normally be perceived by the senses. This realm includes angels, demons and the operation of the Holy Spirit. It also includes God's intervention from time to time through natural disasters.

A Special Type of Political Judgment

Another type of remedial judgment the Bible reveals is that when a nation stubbornly refuses to respond to prophetic voices and the usual types of remedial judgments, God will give the nation the type of leaders it deserves.

This happened to ancient Judah at the end of its history. The people had steadfastly refused to repent, so God gave the nation a king with a depraved mind. His name was Manasseh. He reigned for 55 years. And he proved to be the most evil king in the nation's history (2 Chronicles 33).

In a book published in 2016, titled *Revealed: Obama's Legacy*, Koenig in effect presents President Obama as our nation's Manasseh.[20] He sees him as God's judgment upon America for our descent into secularism and our mistreatment of Israel. In the process, Koenig minces no words:[21]

> The United States of America will never recover from his administration's aggressive assault on Judeo-Christian values and the great damage done to the nation's foundation. This has been a relentless attack in every area that is important to God-fearing and God-believing Christians and Jews.

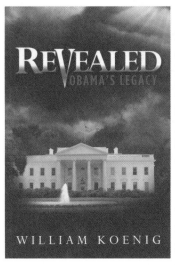

He then adds: "No U.S. Administration has done more to accelerate the nation toward biblical judgment than Obama's."[22] Koenig presents a detailed analysis of Obama's policies to prove his point, presenting as evidence extensive quotes of Obama's own words.

Regarding Islam, Koenig concludes: "No U.S. president or major world leader has done more to promote Islam . . ."[23] He characterizes Obama as "A Muslim Apologist."[25]

Concerning the U.S. military, Koenig argues that "Obama's decisions have decimated the morale of our once-proud military."[26] He points to Obama's purging of generals who disagreed with his policies and likewise his forcing chaplains to leave the military by placing limitations on what they could say and do. Further, he used the military as a social experimental laboratory as he imposed his sexual perversion policies on it.[27]

And speaking of sexual perversion, Koenig asserts:[28]

> No earthly leader has done more to promote the lesbian, gay, bi-sexual, and transgender (LGBT) agenda in the United States and around the world than Barack Obama. He has done more to promote immorality and perverse sexuality than any man in history.

Koenig's greatest disgust with Obama relates to the president's manhandling of Israel from the moment he assumed office. In one sweeping summary sentence, Koenig declares: "The entire Barack Obama presidency was spent undermining

Israel consistently."[29]

And what was the fundamental problem of the Obama Administration? Koenig points to the president's phony Christian faith which was used to cover up his commitment to the fundamentals of Humanism.[30]

> His faith is on his terms. He has said he believes that there are multiple paths to God, not just Christianity. He believes that Allah is the same God of the Christians and Jews . . . He picks and chooses Scriptures that support his beliefs . . . Obama is committed to supplanting Christianity in America . . . Obama actually never wastes an opportunity to marginalize Christianity.

Koenig quotes an observation by comedian Bill Maher, an outspoken atheist, who offered up this interesting observation about Obama's alleged Christian faith: "Obama's really a 'drop dead atheist' pretending to be a Christian." He went on to say that "Obama only joined Reverend Jeremiah Wright's church in Chicago because it was politically necessary."[31]

Koenig's conclusion about Obama's faith is that his "seeming Christianity is in fact a front for his true religious worldview: transforming the West from a freedom-loving community to a neo-Marxist, Islam-friendly 'community organization.'"[32]

The Root of our Problems

Like all of God's prophetic voices speaking to our nation today, Koenig recognizes that the basic issue is God vs Man. Or, to put it another way, is our nation going to repent and turn back to God, or is it going to continue down the suicidal path of making Man its god?

In 2010 in an op-ed column, Koenig stated that "the root cause" of every problem facing our nation today is "personal sin."[33] He continued: "Our nation's leaders are endorsing the most sinful agenda in history," and "public endorsement of sin will result in consequences as grave as in the days of Noah."[34]

In another powerful op-ed written in the same year, Koenig focused in on our nation's Ivy League schools and characterized them as "bastions of Humanism" responsible for supplying the leaders "who are directly responsible for the debacles that we are facing."[35]

He concluded by observing: "Unbeknownst to them, all of these schools are rapidly producing leaders in our country that are leading us to the final days and Jesus Christ's return to Jerusalem," and it is all due to the fact that they have "fallen under the leadership of academic elites whose god is Secular Humanism."[36]

Jan Markell

Chapter 9

Jan Markell:
A Voice Denouncing Apostasy

I solemnly charge you in the presence of God and of Christ Jesus, who is to judge the living and the dead, and by His appearing and His kingdom: preach the word; be ready in season and out of season; reprove, rebuke, exhort, with great patience and instruction. For the time will come when they will not endure sound doctrine; but wanting to have their ears tickled, they will accumulate for themselves teachers in accordance to their own desires, and will turn away their ears from the truth and will turn aside to myths. —

2 Timothy 4:1-4

Jan Markell is truly a "watchman on the wall" (Isaiah 62:6). She loves her Lord and her Church. She boldly asserts that Jesus is the only way to Heaven. And she has dedicated herself to guarding His Church from both internal heresies and external attacks.

She is another very unlikely candidate to serve the Lord as a prophetic voice to our nation. She was born and raised in Minneapolis, Minnesota where she grew up in a home with an Orthodox Jewish father and an elapsed Evangelical mother.[1]

When she was 11 years old, some Christian neighbors

invited her to go with them to a nearby Baptist Church to hear the famous Messianic evangelist named Hyman Appelman (1902-1983). She later said that she was not sure she understood all that he was talking about, "but that man convicted me."[2]

When she shared his message with her mom, she got convicted also and decided to get the both of them active in a church where they could grow in the faith. "We ultimately found a solid Baptist church, and we got very involved."[3] It happened to be a church where Bible prophecy was taught, and so, as a teenager, Jan began to learn God's Prophetic Word.

Getting into Ministry

When she was 30 years old, Markell visited Israel, read Hal Lindsey's *Late Great Planet Earth*, and got involved with Messianic Judaism — all in one year's time![4] For two years she worked with Jews for Jesus. Then, in 1982, she formed her own ministry and called it Olive Tree Ministries.

Those early years of ministry were very busy and exciting:[5]

> When I began Olive Tree Ministries, I ministered in hundreds of churches, home fellowships, women's groups, and even some men's groups. Every week I would pile my small vehicle with a 12 string guitar, sound and audio-visual equipment, books, and a map and head toward destinations large and small. My audiences were enthusiastic as I shared messages focusing on Bible prophecy, Israel, Israel in prophecy, Christ in the Passover, Jewish evangelism and current events.

But this frenetic activity did not last for long. In 1985 she was forced to greatly curtail her ministry due to being afflicted with Chronic Fatigue Syndrome.[6] She battled this condition for 21 years until August of 2000 when she was very suddenly and miraculously healed.[7]

In April of 2001, with her new-found energy, Markell started a radio program on one local station. A year later, she started holding Bible prophecy conferences. As she put it to me in an email message, "I was in my 50s kind of starting over."[8]

Today, her radio program is syndicated on the Salem Radio Network and is broadcast weekly over 850 radio stations. Her annual prophecy conference attracts an audience of 3,000 to 4,000 per day.[9] Her listeners say "Jan is a reality check on the news."[10]

Jan Markell broadcasting a radio program.

When asked if she preferred to be called a Messianic Jew or a Christian Jew, she replied, "I am just a Bible believing Christian with a Jewish heritage."[11]

Her mom died of cancer in 1987. Her dad became a believer in Yeshua in his waning years. Jan spent two years at Bethel University in St. Paul, Minnesota where she earned an Associate degree. She has never married. Her ministry headquarters is located in Maple Grove, Minnesota, a suburb of Minneapolis.

Jan Markell is a strong woman with strong opinions, but one interesting thing I discovered is that she often expresses her opinions through other people. She does this through the people she invites to speak at her conferences, through those she selects to interview on the radio, and through the authors she quotes extensively in her articles.

Israel in Theology

Being Jewish and a student of Bible prophecy, Markell has always been a staunch advocate in behalf of Israel and the Jewish people.

Like Bill Koenig, she has been an outspoken opponent of Replacement Theology. She has verbally blasted the Presbyterian Church USA, the Episcopal Church, the United Methodist Church, and the Evangelical Lutheran Church for their criticism of Israel and their support of the Palestinians.[12] She has also rebuked the World and National Councils of Churches, proclaiming that "ecumenism is their real god."[13]

Markell takes the position that when a person or church embraces Replacement Theology, they end up with "replacement reality" because "reality gets totally skewed."[14] She argues that the refusal to recognize the re-establishment of Israel as part of God's end time plan is "all a part of the end time falling away the Bible predicts" will be a part of the rampant apostasy that will characterize the final days before Jesus returns.[15] She says she knows there are some good people in these churches, "but for the sake of your soul and your family, may I urge you to flee unless you feel you can make a difference."[16]

Markell has also taken a strong stand against another heretical doctrine that relates to the Jewish people. It is called Dual Covenant Theology. This is the absurd idea that the Jewish people do not need Jesus because they can be saved by following the laws of the Torah. She has declared that this viewpoint amounts to loving the Jews into Hell.[17]

She tells about attending "a night to honor Israel" at a Word of Faith church in the Minneapolis/St. Paul area. The pastor of the church ended the program by telling the audience of Jews and Christians that the Jews do not need to be saved because they are "automatically saved." She labeled the pastor a "Pied Piper of Heresy," and she said this "night to honor Israel should have been labeled 'a night to curse the Jews.'"[18] She concluded the article by observing that "ushering the Jewish people into Hell by withholding the Gospel is hardly blessing them or doing them a favor."[19]

Israel in Politics

Markell gets absolutely livid when commenting on Israel's mistreatment by our nation or in the realm of international politics. She thoroughly condemned President Obama's deal with Iran in 2015, arguing that he had "lit the first match for World War III which will morph into Armageddon."[20] She declared that it was "the deal from Hell" and that Obama was nothing but "an agent of the ayatollahs."[21]

In like manner, she blasted Obama for his decision in December 2016 to lift the U.S. veto in the U.N. Security Council in order to allow the passage of a resolution of condemnation of Israel for building new apartments in disputed territory. This resolution also affirmed Palestinian authority over East Jerusalem, including the Temple Mount and the Western Wall within the Old City.[22]

Markell blamed Obama for the resolution, saying it was just another attempt on his part to "humiliate and marginalize" Israel's Prime Minister Bibi Nethanyahu.[23] She likewise castigated the United Nations, branding it as "the most corrupt, tin-pot-dictator-driven, anti-American, anti-Semitic, American-resource-draining cesspool in the world."[24]

Concern for the Church

God's purposes among the Jewish people are central to Markell, but an even greater passion of hers is the purity of the Lord's Church. This is the topic she has focused on in recent years, particularly due to the increasing influence of the apostate Emergent Church Movement.

In a recent email message to me, she stated, "My real burden today is the state of the Church."[25] She went on to say that she is "heartbroken" over what is happening to the Church today. "I have memories of the church of my youth," she wrote, ". . . a church that was so solid, was prophecy and Israel focused, and talked about important things, not 'seeker-sensitive' issues."[26]

The Erosion of the Evangelical Movement

The logo
of Markell's ministry.

Markell has pointed out repeatedly that the term, Evangelical, no longer has any meaning. At one time it stood for people who believed in the inerrancy of the Bible and believed the Bible should be our guide for all doctrines and morals. Today there are people calling themselves Evangelicals who are denying the fundamentals of the faith. In fact, the apostasy among Evangelicals has grown so great that it is now often difficult to differentiate them from the old mainline denominational liberal advocates of the Social Gospel.[27]

In a powerful article titled, "Liberal Evangelicals Don't Represent Me," Markell points out that in 2006 "Evangelicals jumped on the global-warming bandwagon." In 2010, "immigration became the new Evangelical cause." In 2011, came the "Circle of Protection" made up of those Evangelicals who were focused on protecting the poor from federal budget cuts. The climax came later that year when the National Association of Evangelicals decided to call for nuclear disarmament.[28]

In another article, Markell stated that "on the surface there doesn't seem to be a dime's worth of difference between the National Association of Evangelicals and the World and National Councils of Churches."[29] She added:[30]

> For years the NAE focused on salvation issues. Not any longer . . . The NAE's most recent press release . . . is their endorsement of "An Evangelical Declaration Against Torture." Tell them you want an "Evangelical Declaration on Saving Lost Souls."

"Christians should care about the poor," wrote Markell, "but to me, poverty, climate change, war, immigration and women's rights are not primary Evangelical issues."[31] Instead, she argued, "Evangelicals should be focused on soul winning:"[32]

> Once again, we see a vain "fix the earth" mentality. The wrongs of this world cannot be made right until Christ's return. Since that just might be soon, could we please go back to the fundamentals of soul winning, the calling card of Evangelicals for decades? We can't fix anything on this planet because the devil is in charge right now. One of the things our government is assigned to do, and rightly so, is to protect its citizens. One of the things Evangelicals are to do is to share the Gospel. Nuclear disarmament is not a church issue. Somebody do a reality check.

In another article titled, "When Evangelicals Dine With The Wicked," Markell castigated Bill Hybels, the founder of the "seeker-sensitive" approach to Christianity.[33] She emphasized his annual "leadership conferences" that have featured "problematic" speakers like Jimmy Carter, Tony Blair and rock star Bono — among many others.

In response, Markell asked a series of penetrating questions:[34]

> Will these speakers spur the attendees to share their faith with greater zeal?

How will the attendees grow spiritually from their exposure to these people?

How does this further the Kingdom of God?

Emergent Church Leaders

Markell has also written extensively about the dangers of the Emergent Church Movement and its leaders. She has called the movement a "dangerous fad" that is helping to undermine our nation's Judeo-Christian worldview.[35]

This movement emphasizes mysticism, sensory immersion and opinions as opposed to biblical truths. In fact, many of its leaders would deny the existence of absolute truth. Many also denigrate the all-sufficiency of the Scriptures.

Some of Markell's revelations about the movement include the following:

- The most visible leader of the movement, Brian McLaren, has stated "that not all people need to be Christians to follow Jesus — some may be Buddhists or Hindu followers."[36]

- Richard Foster and Brennan Manning, both revered by Evangelicals, "have never met a mystical practice they didn't endorse."[37]

- *Christianity Today* magazine, supposedly the "house organ of Evangelicalism," called the *Harry Potter* books "a wonderful Christmas gift for all."[38]

- Markell's alma mater, Bethel University in St. Paul, Minnesota, claims to be an Evangelical school that is dedicated to "taking our faith in Christ and integrating it into everything we learn . . ."[39] Yet, in 2009, the university sponsored an "Interreligious Symposium" promoting common ground between Buddhism and

Christianity. Markell wrote the conference off with these words: "Bethel University throws it students to interspiritual wolves."[40]

Rick Warren

Markell has been particularly aggravated with Rick Warren, the highly influential pastor of the Saddleback Church in Lake Forest, California. She has focused on him because of his widespread influence among Evangelicals.

In 2009, she posted an "open letter" to Rick Warren in response to his appearance before the Islamic Society of North America (ISNA).[41] According to the *Washington Times*, Warren told that group that he envisions "a coalition of faith."[42] The *Times* also reported that "Mr. Warren was sparse in his mentions of Jesus and God."[43]

In her open letter to Warren, Markell stated:[44]

Pastor Warren, you pleaded with 8,000 Muslim listeners . . . to work together to solve the world's greatest problems by cooperating in a series of interfaith projects. You said, "Muslims and Christians can work together for the common good without compromising my convictions or your convictions."

Pastor Warren, you needed to compromise the convictions of the Muslims in attendance. The hour is too late to withhold a Gospel message without which they will face a Christless eternity, and you will be held accountable . . . I have to conclude that you are more interested in ecumenical unity and solving AIDS, poverty and other social issues . . . You were given a golden opportunity that 99% of American Christians could never get.

Markell also noted in the open letter that Warren had been one of the Evangelical leaders who had signed the Yale University document in 2008 that apologized to Muslims "for all the evil deeds perpetrated against them by Christians."[45] She characterized his endorsement of that document as "pandering" and making himself "sound like a fool."[46] She concluded her letter by saying, "It seems to me that you are more interested in marching hand-in-hand with other faiths down the winding road to the coming one-world religion."[47]

In January of 2011, Markell published another article about Warren which began with the question: "What on earth is Pastor Rick Warren thinking?"[48] She then outlined the reasons for her question:[49]

- Praising Syria for its "religious freedom."

- Sharing church-growth principles with synagogues.

- Being part of the leadership team or board of advisors to questionable organizations such as The World Economic Forum, The Council on Foreign Relations and Tony Blair's Faith Foundation.

- Misquoting Jesus in *The Purpose Driven Life* by saying that He stated, "My return is none of your business," when, in fact, the Bible emphasizes that His return is our "blessed hope" (Titus 2:13).

- Embracing Kingdom Now/Dominion eschatology which says the Church will save the world through Warren's global P.E.A.C.E. Plan — when we are on a cursed earth that only Christ's return can save.

- Underplaying the issues of Hell, sin and repentance in his books.

Criticism

Some Christian spokesmen have responded to Markell by condemning her for criticizing fellow Christian leaders — and in particular for naming them.

But how is the person in the pew supposed to deal with apostasy if they are unaware of those who are spreading it? The Apostle Paul was certainly not reticent about identifying the apostate teachers in his day. He named Hymenaeus and Alexander (1 Timothy 1:20), Phygelus and Hermogenes (2 Timothy 1:15), Hymenaeus and Philetus (2 Timothy 2:17) and Alexander the metalworker (2 Timothy 4:14). Paul even criticized Peter publicly for being hypocritical by living as a Gentile while insisting that Gentiles live as Jews (Galatians 2:11-14).

The critics always respond by quoting Matthew 7:1 which says, "Do not judge so that you will not be judged." This passage must be referring to the judgment of motives, not words and actions. The fact of the matter is that Christians have an obligation to judge words and actions because the Bible commands us to test everything by the Word (Galatians 1:8-9 and 1 John 4:1). It is impossible to test something without judging it.

Paul complimented the brethren in Berea for testing his teachings by the Word of God (Acts 17:10-11). Likewise, Jesus commended the Church in Ephesus for testing self-proclaimed "apostles" whom He called liars (Revelation 2:2).

Mike Oppenheimer, a Messianic Jew who has an apologetics ministry called "Let Us Reason," has addressed this issue in detail. He has written, "To watch our spiritual family being misled is negligence and is absence of true compassion."[50] "True love" he adds, "is not silent when people are being misled, hurt or abused." He concludes:[51]

It is right to expose error and to name those who are teaching error. Faithful messengers will warn the sheep of heresy, and when needed, identify them by name.

The author with Jan Markell at one of her conferences.

The Relationship to Our Nation

So, how does apostasy in the Church relate to the disintegration of our nation? Because the Church is supposed to stand for righteousness, condemn evil, call for repentance and preach the Gospel. Our society is falling apart because the Church has stopped doing these things. In its desire to be accepted by the world, the Church has gotten in bed with the world, embracing the world's demand for tolerance of all kinds of evils.

Addressing this fact, Markell has written:[52]

God raised this . . . nation up for several reasons. We have been a Gospel light to the world . . . We have been Israel's "off-and-on" ally. Our Christian heritage has made us a compassionate nation. But I see a nation pulling away from the one true God and

giving a voice to those who hate God or who
have a skewed view of Him.

As evidence of what she calls "the great falling away,"
Markell printed a list in January of 2008 of events in 2007
that evidenced an abandonment of the Judeo-Christian consensus this nation was founded on:[53]

- The Congressional Gold Medal was granted to
  the Dalai Lama.

- A Hindu opened the U.S. Senate with a prayer.

- A Muslim delivered a prayer in the U.S. House
  of Representatives.

- A nationwide emphasis was placed on interfaith gatherings.

- Atheists became increasingly aggressive in their
  attack on God and Christianity.

- President Bush stated that "all religions pray to
  the same God."

- The lead story in *US News & World Report* at
  the end of 2007 was about Protestants returning
  to Catholicism.

Christian apostates are not the only ones Markell blames
for America's demise. Like the other prophetic voices God
has raised up, she points to the proponents of Humanism,
calling them "Masters of Deceit."[54]

The Future

Despite all her passionate concerns about the Church and
American society, Markell does not despair.

One of the fundamental themes that runs through all her
articles is: "Things Aren't Falling Apart — They Are Falling
In Place!"[55] This observation is based on the many Bible

prophecies that state that the end times will be characterized by apostasy in the Church and immorality, violence and chaos in society (2 Thessalonians 2:3 and 2 Timothy 3:1-5). Jesus Himself said that when He returns, society will be as evil as it was in the days of Noah (Matthew 24:37).

With regard to "things falling into place," Markell has declared:[56]

> Humpty Dumpty is having a great fall, but secular mankind cannot figure out how to put him back together. They think new elections, new laws, new treaties and new regulations will fix everything! They are clueless that the secular path always leads to folly . . .

> We have passed the tipping point. Let's hang on a little longer and be salt and light and try to delay the decay. There are still some faithful shepherds in some of our pulpits . . . Nothing is falling apart. Everything is falling in place. More distress is coming, and it will be heart-stopping and breathtaking. Judgment is upon us.

But Markell rarely ever ends one of her articles on a negative note. She usually concludes by emphasizing that although the world is facing unprecedented turmoil, Christians have a glorious hope based on the promises of God. A typical ending for her is this one:[57]

> While we may be on the brink of global chaos, the true believer can take comfort in the fact that we are also on the brink of Jesus' glorious return.

Albert Mohler, Jr.

Chapter 10

Albert Mohler, Jr.: A Voice Confronting Intellectuals

See to it that no one takes you captive through philosophy and empty deception, according to the tradition of men, according to the elementary principles of the world, rather than according to Christ. — Colossians 2:8

In 1993 the Southern Baptist Theological Seminary in Louisville, Kentucky, faced a major crisis. Ever since the 1960s the school had experienced a shift to the left, with an ever increasing number of professors espousing liberal theology. The Southern Baptist Convention had replaced the school's Board of Trustees with conservative, Bible-believing members who were fed up with the school's drift away from orthodox Baptist theology. This action had set the stage for a major confrontation.

To illustrate how bad the situation was, Bryant Wright was a student at Southern in the late 1970s. He currently serves as pastor of Johnson Ferry Baptist Church in Marietta, Georgia. He served as President of the Southern Baptist Convention from 2010 to 2012. In a video interview shot in 2013 he reminisced about his days at Southern in the late 70s and early 80s.

He said that during his first year at Southern, one of the faculty members asked him, "You don't really believe that you have to believe in the bodily resurrection of Jesus Christ to be a Christian, do you?" He said he was astounded by the question and thought the professor was kidding him. But he was not. When Wright responded that he thought a belief in the resurrection of Jesus was essential, the professor shot back, "Well, after you've been here six months to a year, you will get over all that!"[1]

Dr. Timothy George, who serves as the Dean of Beeson Divinity School in Alabama has summed up the theological drift that happened at Southern in these highly academic words: "There was an aspirational gravitation toward more mainline, accepted, accommodated, acculturated forms of Christianity."[2] Translated, that means there was a purposeful attempt to line up the theology taught by Southern with the liberal Social Gospel of the historical mainline denominations like the Presbyterians, Methodists and Episcopalians.

A Crucial Decision

To the astonishment of everyone, the Board of Trustees of Southern decided to place the fate of the institution in the hands of a 33 year old man named Albert Mohler, Jr. Mohler was a staunch conservative who believed in biblical inerrancy and who strongly affirmed the fundamentals of the faith.

His selection was a sure sign by the board that they meant business. But the faculty dug in, and the war lines were drawn. Within two years of Mohler's appointment, in 1995, the faculty voted almost unanimously in favor of a motion that rebuked him and repudiated his policies. Only four members voted in his favor.[3] One of the opposing faculty members who later left the school has since referred to Mohler as "a Baptist version of the Taliban."[4]

Mohler has since written that on that day, he "thought it was all over."[5] He said he was "completely spent."[6] He went home, embraced his wife, Mary, and the two of them "cried together."[7]

Mohler at his desk. Notice the bust of Winston Churchill in the foreground. Mohler is considered to be an expert on the life of Churchill.
(https://baptistnews.com)

The Man

Who was this young man who created such a volatile reaction? Albert Mohler, Jr., was born in Lakeland, Florida in 1959. He grew up there. He was characterized by intellectual curiosity from the word go. He kept a record of the books he had read, and by the time he was a senior in high school, he had read more than 80 — many of which were heavy-weight volumes on theology.

During his junior year in high school, he says he experienced an "apologetic crisis" that continued for two years until he discovered the writings of Francis Schaeffer. He says that Schaeffer's books proved to be "a form of theological rescue" for him.[8]

After graduation from high school, Mohler was selected as a Faculty Scholar at Florida Atlantic University. He later transferred to Samford University, a Baptist-affiliated college in Birmingham, Alabama. In 1980, at the age of 21, he moved to Louisville and became a graduate student at Southern Seminary. Between 1980 and 1989, when he earned his doctorate, he worked at the seminary in various fund-raising positions.[9] In 1989 he became the editor of *The Christian Index*, a bi-weekly newsletter of the Georgia Baptist Convention, and he continued in that capacity until he was appointed president of Southern in 1993.[10]

Throwing Down the Gauntlet

When Mohler arrived on the Southern campus as the new president, he acted immediately to make it clear that he intended to clean the house of liberal professors. He called a convocation and delivered a message that his opponents dubbed, "A Declaration of War."[11] He declared that the school had lost its way theologically and needed to recommit with integrity to its confession of faith which was called, "The Abstract of Principles."

Every professor was required to sign this creedal statement, but there had been a custom for many years that allowed each person to interpret the meaning of the statement as he or she pleased. Mohler made it crystal clear that this would no longer be tolerated. During the ensuing months, when it became apparent that he meant what he said, the faculty revolted, leading up to the no-confidence vote in 1995.

This led to campus protests by students who demanded Mohler's resignation. Students refused to shake his hand at graduation when he presented them with their diplomas, and one even spat on him.

But the Board of Trustees stood firm. They endorsed his demand that all faculty sign the institution's creedal statement with no stated or mental reservations. They also adopted an early retirement package as an "exit plan for liberal faculty to leave."[12]

Throughout the painful ordeal, Mohler continued to affirm that his purpose "was to see Southern Seminary unapologetically committed to the faith once and for all delivered to the saints, to the service of the Southern Baptist Convention, to an affirmation of biblical inerrancy and a passion for the Gospel."[13]

Since that time, God has richly blessed the seminary. The student body now exceeds 3,000, making Southern the second largest seminary of its kind.[14] The finances of the school are more secure than ever before. The budget has doubled and the endowment has grown to more than $30 million.[15] And Mohler says every faculty member now signs the school's confession of faith "with gladness of heart."[16]

A Growing Reputation

Since those chaotic days, Mohler has emerged as what *Time* magazine has called the "reigning intellectual of the Evangelical Movement in the U.S."[17] It is a title that is well deserved.

Accordingly, his books are difficult to read and understand because they are aimed at theological and philosophical intellectuals, and that is a service that the Evangelical Movement

Mohler doing his radio program, "The Briefing."
(www.stitcher.com)

desperately needs. But Mohler also speaks to the general population through articles he writes for his Internet blog, and he hosts a daily podcast called "The Briefing," which he uses to present a biblical perspective on current events and cultural issues.[18]

One thing is for sure — Mohler is not some aloof and stuffy intellectual. As evidence, he has written:

"Jesus loves me — this I know, for the Bible tells me so." A mature Christian faith

will say more than that, not less than that.
"For the Bible tells me so" does not mean that
we do not have reasoned answers to difficult
questions, but it does mean that we admit our
dependence on Scripture — and that we confess that God intended for us to be dependent
on Scriptures.

Mohler has also established himself as a major prophetic
voice, pointing to the failures of both the Church and society
and warning of the dire consequences of rebellion against
God. In fact, he has articulated one of the most insightful
statements concerning the peril our nation currently faces.
This summary was presented in a profound speech that he
made at Brigham Young University in February of 2014:[19]

I come in what can only be described as a
dangerous moment for us all and for the culture and civilization we commonly love. The
most fundamental values of civilization itself
are threatened, and we are witnesses to one of
the most comprehensive and fast-paced moral
revolutions ever experienced by humanity.
The velocity and breadth of this revolution are
breathtaking, and the consequences are yet
incalculable.

This society is dismantling the very structures that have allowed for the enjoyment and
preservation of human liberty and respect for
life. We are engaged in a head-long effort to
replace the convictions that gave birth to
democracy and ordered liberty with a new set
of convictions that will lead to the emergence
of a very different culture, society and civilization.

> We cannot pretend that this is not happen-
> ing. We cannot delude ourselves into believ-
> ing that it will not matter.

Mohler proceeded to point out that Karl Marx had prophesied that "the modern age would sweep all conventional
morality and political structures aside in a complete transfor-
mation of values." Mohler than declared, "What Marx promised is now happening before our eyes."[20]

And then Mohler asked the basic question: "What can
explain it?" I found it fascinating that he answered the
question by reaching back to one of the prophets featured in
Part 1 of this book: "That great Russian prophet, Aleksandr
Solzhenitsyn, explained it with four simple words — 'Men
have forgotten God.'" "And so they have," Mohler affirmed,
adding, "Nothing else can explain the great shift in worldview
we are witnessing."[21]

An Overview of Mohler's Writings

Mohler's writings are so voluminous and comprehensive
that it would be impossible to present a definitive survey of
them in one short chapter. So, what I will do is give you a
taste of them by subject matter.

Freedom of Religion

To illustrate how fast the attitude toward religious freedom has shifted in our society, Mohler reminds us of the
Federal Religious Freedom Restoration Act that was enacted
by Congress in 1993. It passed the House of Representatives
unanimously and received 97 of 100 votes in the Senate. It
was signed into law by President Bill Clinton who declared
religious liberty to be the nation's "first freedom."[22] Yet, only
23 years later in 2016, when Hillary Clinton launched her
presidential campaign, she condemned the law as "dangerous
and discriminatory."[23] That is a startling shift in a very short
time.

Mohler also points out that both President Obama and the *New York Times* have emphasized that the Constitution protects only "freedom of worship" — which, translated, means religious liberty is limited to what happens in a church, temple, mosque or synagogue.[24] Mohler warns that if religious liberty is reduced to a private sphere with no public voice, the very freedom to preach the Gospel of Jesus Christ will be at stake. "If we lose religious liberty, all other liberties will be lost, one by one."[25]

Sexual Freedom

Mohler has constantly warned that the release of sexuality from all inhibitions and moral norms poses a great threat to Christian liberties. As he rightfully projected, this trend has led to a conflict of liberties, and the courts and the state have sided with the sexual libertarians. The ominous result is that "erotic liberty has been elevated as a right more fundamental than religious liberty."[26] And he proceeds to point out many different ways in which a stand for religious liberty could end up putting Christians in jail.

Vulgarity

"The collapse of the barrier between popular culture and decadence has released a toxic mudslide of vulgarity into the nation's family rooms — and just about everywhere else. There is almost no remote corner of this culture that is not marked by the toleration of vulgarity, or the outright celebration of depravity."[27] The bottom line is that "a culture afraid to repress sexuality in any way is a culture headed to destruction."[28]

Homosexuality

Mohler sees this issue as a pivotal one. He says it will determine whether Evangelicals will remain true to the teachings of Scripture, or whether they will cave in to the demands of a depraved society.[29] He asserts that the mainline, liberal denominations have already surrendered. But what concerns him the most is that "the seams in the Evangelical fabric are beginning to break."[30] He argues that we have already reached the point where "homophobia is now the new mental illness and moral deficiency, while homosexuality is accepted as the new normal."[31]

Mohler contends that this is a "critical watershed issue" because it puts the veracity of the Bible at stake.[32] Mohler strongly asserts that the biblical witness is clear: "Homosexuality is a sin against God and a direct rejection of God's intention and command in creation."[33] He concludes that "in the end, the Church will either declare the truth of God's Word, or it will find a way to run from it."[34]

Same-Sex Marriage

Mohler argues that Christians should not oppose same-sex marriage only because we believe it is contrary to Scripture, but also because "we believe that anything opposed to Scripture cannot lead to human flourishing."[35] He then explains that "if we misunderstand or misrepresent what sin is, we undercut the work of Christ and our knowledge of the fact that we need a Savior."[36]

R. Albert Mohler, Jr.

WE CANNOT BE SILENT

Speaking truth to a culture redefining sex, marriage, & the very meaning of right & wrong

In 2010 when a federal judge arbitrarily threw out Proposition 8, which had been affirmed by a majority of California voters to define marriage as the union of a man and a woman, Mohler called the decision "one brazen act of judicial energy."[37] He predicted that this decision would ultimately lead to a "direct hit" on the "central institution of human civilization."[38]

When the same-sex marriage case was argued before the Supreme Court in May of 2015, Mohler expressed great concern over the responses of the Obama Administration's attorney to the questions of the judges — not questions about same-sex marriage, but about the implications of the legalization of such a biblical perversion. The Solicitor General, Daniel Verrilli, made it clear that the legalization of same-sex marriage would "put the nation's religious institutions, including Christian colleges, schools and seminaries on notice."[39] In one of his responses to a question from Justice Alito, Verrilli even indicated that the government might challenge the tax-exempt status of any organization that refused to abide by the Court's decision.[40]

When the Court issued its abominable decision on June 26, 2015 in which it legalized same-sex marriage, Mohler immediately issued a press release that began with the enigmatic statement: "Everything has changed and nothing has changed."[41] He characterized the Court's decision "as an act of will disguised as a legal judgment."[42] He ended by explaining his opening sentence:[43]

> In one sense, everything has changed. And yet, nothing has changed. The cultural and legal landscape has changed, as we believe this will lead to very real harms to our neighbors. But our Christian responsibility has not changed. We are charged to uphold marriage as the union of a man and a woman and to speak the truth in love. We are also commanded to uphold the truth about marriage in our own lives, In our own marriages, in our own families, and in our own churches.

Pornography

In response to the book and movie, *Fifty Shades of Grey*, Mohler became rather theological. He began by asserting that one of the hallmarks of the Christian worldview is an "affirmation of the unity of the . . . good, the beautiful and the true," which are unified in their source — "God Himself, who alone is infinitely good, beautiful and true."[44] He then points out that "Christians believe the radical truth that nothing good can be ugly, that nothing untrue can be beautiful, and that everything beautiful and true is also good."[45] Therefore, "any attempt to declare beauty at the expense of goodness and truth is at the heart of the problem of pornography."[46]

He then abandoned the theology and got down to the nitty-gritty, claiming that the explosion of pornography in our society is evidence of a "lost sense of shame."[47] And whereas modern society sees this as "cultural progress," it really "points to the depth of the confusion that inevitably accompanies the corruption of God's gifts."[48]

Abortion

"The tragedy of abortion remains one of this nation's greatest reasons for shame, and the fact that over a million abortions are performed each year is nothing less than horrifying."[49] At the "epicenter of the 'Culture of Death' stands Planned Parenthood."[50] It is an "abortion industrial complex" that is funded by our tax dollars. "The group thrives because Americans allow it to thrive."[51] And the horrifying exposure that the organization has been involved in harvesting baby hearts for sale should "lead to our own broken hearts. A nation that will allow this, will allow anything."[52]

Doctrinal Purity

Mohler has been a vigilant protector of the fundamentals of the faith. A good example is the strong defense he has presented in behalf of the Virgin Birth — one of Christendom's most attacked doctrines, both from without and within Christianity.

In an article written in 2011, Mohler asked, "Can a Christian, once aware of the Bible's teaching, reject the Virgin Birth?" His response: "The answer must be no."[53]

Again, he points to the real issue as being the veracity of the Bible: "We cannot claim to believe the Bible is the Word of God and then turn around and cast suspicion on its teaching."[54] Mohler states that the Virgin Birth is essential to the faith because "it explains how Christ could be both God and man, how He was without sin."[55]

Conclusion

So, considering the rapid deterioration of our society and the increasing apostasy in the Church, what are we as Christians to do?

The title of one of Mohler's books provides the answer: *We Cannot Be Silent* (2015). He wraps up the book with the following observations:[56]

> We must contend for marriage as God's gift to humanity . . . We must contend for religious liberty for all.

> We cannot be silent, and we cannot join the moral revolution that stands in direct opposition to what we believe the Creator has designed, given and intended for us . . .

> We are called to be the people of the truth, even when the truth is not popular and even when the truth is denied by the culture around us . . .

> The holy Scriptures have not changed. The Gospel of Jesus Christ has not changed. The Church's mission has not changed. Jesus Christ is the same, yesterday, today and forever.

Franklin Graham

Chapter 11

Franklin Graham: A Voice Calling for Repentance

Righteousness exalts a nation, But sin is a disgrace to any people. — Proverbs 14:34

In 1991 an outstanding academic biography of Billy Graham was published. It was titled, *A Prophet With Honor.*[1] The author, Dr. William Martin, was at that time a professor at Rice University where he specialized in the sociology of religion.

I knew Dr. Martin personally since we had been students together at Harvard University in the early 1960s. As soon as the book was published, I called him and asked, "Why in the world did you title the book, *A Prophet With Honor*? You know as well as I do that Billy Graham was anything but a prophet!"

Dr. Martin laughed and responded, "Yes, Dave, I realize that, but in like manner, you know as well as I do that publishers demand absolute control over a book's cover and its title." He went on to explain that he had engaged in a wrestling match with the publisher over the title, but had lost.

A Difference in Styles and Callings

Billy Graham was a very gifted and effective evangelist, but he certainly was no prophet. He sought the favor of politicians, he tried to avoid offending anyone, and he had "an obsessive need for approval."[2] His son, Franklin, has summed it up this way: "Daddy hates to say no. I can say no."[3]

In stark contrast, Franklin could care less about currying the favor of politicians, he refuses to tip-toe through the tulips with regard to controversial issues, and he seeks no one's approval except the Lord's. "I've never really been one to try to be politically correct," Franklin has stated. "I just feel truth is truth, and sometimes I probably offend some people."[4]

Well, as we shall see, there is no "probably" about it. Franklin drives his critics crazy with his refusal to compromise on the issues, and as a result, he is the focus of unrelenting attacks. Take, for example the headline of a *Huffington Post* article dated March 6, 2015: "Franklin Graham is Still the Worst Thing to Happen to God in a While."[5] The author of the article proclaimed, "God has a tough time living down Franklin Graham's narrow bigotry."[6]

Franklin is not a chip off the old block. His focus and

Franklin Graham with is father.
(Photo courtesy of the Billy Graham Evangelistic Association)

style are radically different from his father's. Franklin has commented about their differences several times in public. He has pointed out that he has received criticism from both Christian leaders and staff members that could be summed up with the words, "Your father would never have said that or taken that position in public."[7]

Franklin normally responds to such observations by pointing out that his father ministered in a Christian nation whereas he is ministering in the midst of a nation that is jettisoning its Christian heritage.[8]

That observation is legitimate, but it does not explain the major differences in their ministries. Those differences are rooted in their gifting by the Holy Spirit. Billy was gifted as an evangelist, and he used that gift mightily to proclaim the Gospel to more people than any other evangelist who has ever lived. Franklin, on the other hand, has been gifted prophetically, and he is thus more concerned with speaking out against the evils of society and calling people to repentance.

The spiritual gift of prophecy can be manifested in three ways:

1) Supernatural knowledge of the future.

2) The ability to understand and teach Bible prophecy.

3) The ability and compulsion to apply the Scriptures to contemporary national and international issues.

Franklin Graham excels in the third category, and like his father who preached the Gospel boldly and without compromise, Franklin speaks out fearlessly on all the social and moral issues of our time, calling our nation to repentance and righteousness.

Early History

But a commitment to righteousness has not always been the case in Franklin's life, as indicated by the title of his autobiography, *Rebel With a Cause: Finally Comfortable Being Graham* (1995).[9] Likewise, the CNN biographical sketch on its website is titled, "The Prodigal Son Comes Home."[10] The biography on the CBS website has a similar title, "Franklin Graham: The hell-raising evangelist's son."[11]

William Franklin Graham, III, was born in 1952. He was the fourth of five children born to Billy Graham and his wife, Ruth. At that time, his family lived in a log house in the Appalachian Mountains outside Asheville, North Carolina.[12] He was basically raised by his mother since his father was always on the road preaching. He admired his mother's adventurous spirit and sense of humor.[13]

Franklin was a mischievous boy who loved to hunt and fish. His "boyhood mischief grew into adult rebellion. He rode motorcycles, learned how to pilot planes and lived life in the fast lane."[14] He smoked, drank, partied with girls and got into fights. CBS commentator, Byron Pitts, summed him up as having the "poster child preacher kid attitude."[15] "It was rebellion against God," Franklin once said. He added, "I wanted to be free, and I wanted to have fun."[16]

The turning point came when his father confronted him one day saying, "I want you to know that your mother and I sense there is a struggle for the soul of your life, and you're going to have to make a choice."[17] Those words penetrated

Franklin's heart, and shortly thereafter, while in a hotel room in Jerusalem, Franklin decided to give his life to Jesus. It was 1974, and Franklin was 22 years old. When he returned home, he announced his new commitment to God, married his hometown girlfriend, Jane, and began looking for ways to serve the Lord.[18]

This was when a family friend, Bob Pierce, the founder of the World Vision and Samaritan's Purse relief ministries, invited Franklin to go on a six week mission tour in Asia. When Pierce died four years later, Franklin took over the leadership of Samaritan's Purse.[19]

In 1989 Franklin reluctantly began speaking in his father's crusades. As he did so, he says he began to realize that his reluctance to become an evangelist was due to the fact that he feared being compared to his father.[20] In the year 2000, Franklin was named the chief executive officer of the Billy Graham Evangelistic Association.

Franklin earned an associate degree from Montreat College and a bachelor's degree from Appalachian State University. He and his wife have three sons and a daughter and eleven grandchildren. They reside in Boone, North Carolina.[21]

An American Prophet

Since 1989, when Franklin began speaking in evangelistic crusades, he has emerged as one of America's most significant prophetic voices, calling this nation to repentance and warning of God's judgment if we fail to repent. He has also established himself as one of the Church's most courageous voices as he speaks out boldly against the sins of our nation.

In sermon after sermon, Franklin has made it clear that he believes America is a nation in revolt against the very One who has blessed it so abundantly. As evidence of the rebellion, he has pointed to the sexual revolution of the 1960s which he says, "left behind a shattered moral landscape that has undermined the fabric and foundation of our nation."[22] He argues that the so-called "freedoms" promised by the sexual revolution have resulted instead in "increasing slavery and captivity to sin."[23]

While commenting on the demands of the LGBT advocacy groups, Franklin presented a sweeping summary of the cultural war that is being waged in America today:[24]

> This is a full-scale assault against Christianity and the followers of Christ. When prayer is banned from the public square; when our President fails to defend biblically defined marriage, and he openly and zealously advocates for gay rights; when legislators rush to overrule existing laws to promote gay marriage; when schools and courts consistently suppress religious freedoms; we know we are locked in a war against the Christian faith, not culture. The architect behind this offensive is none other than Satan himself. The Scripture says that the devil, our archenemy is bent on as much destruction as possible.

Bemoaning the tidal wave of immorality that has swept across our nation since the 1960s, Franklin writes, "There is virtually no place where its corrosive influence is not felt . . Today, what our society seems to value most is the freedom to do whatever makes us feel good."[25] He then observed that anyone who would try to stop Americans from doing destructive things to themselves "is mocked and vilified."[26]

To summarize the moral decay of our nation, Franklin presents the following observation: "The moral compass that once guided our nation's people has been ridiculed and rejected, making sin the national sport and pastime."[27]

The Sources of Our Problems

Franklin puts much of the blame for America's wretched spiritual condition on "sinful entertainment" that "deposits rubbish in the mind, giving Satan a foothold in our lives."[28] Referring to Hollywood as "Follywood," he laments the fact that "we are willing to spend our hard-earned money on . . . films that instill in us the opposite of what the Bible commands."[29]

And with regard to television, Franklin asks, "Why do we welcome into our homes the flaunting of sin that glorifies the flesh and curses the Name of Jesus, while on Sundays we glorify Him at church?"[30] Franklin has stated that when he was a boy, the most risque thing he remembers seeing on TV was Miss Kitty on *Gunsmoke*.[31] But in contrast, "Now even watching the advertisements on television or viewing the trailers for movies is enough to make you blush."[32]

Franklin reserves his most stinging rebuke for what he considers to be the fundamental source of our national spiritual morass — namely, silent pulpits. In May of 2014 he delivered a powerful condemnation of Evangelical pastors and challenged them to rise up and start speaking out in behalf of righteousness.[33]

The occasion was a banquet in Washington, D.C. sponsored by the Family Research Council at which Franklin was given the "Watchman on the Wall Award." He began his remarks by reading Revelation 21:8 where there is a list of eight groups of people who will be consigned to Hell. He pointed out that the very first group mentioned was the "cowardly," and he then launched into a no-holds-barred condemnation of preachers for their cowardice in failing to speak out about the sins of America.[34] He chastised them for evading moral issues for fear of offending someone:[35]

> Christians cannot ignore parts of God's
> Word because they are unpopular or cause

division. Our commission is to proclaim
Christ and all He stands for. This is what the
church's presence in the world is all about.
We cannot sincerely proclaim the truth of
God's love while ignoring what He hates, and
God hates sin.

He proceeded to point out that just as our nation has
drifted from the strict interpretation of the Constitution, so
also has the church seriously drifted from taking God at His
Word.[36] He added, "It is cowardice to excuse sin by claiming
[as do many preachers] we have no right to judge what God
has already judged." He referred his audience to the words of
Isaiah 51:7,13 which reads: "Listen to Me, you who know
righteousness, you people in whose heart is My law: Do not
fear the reproach of men, nor be afraid of their insults . . .
You have feared continually every day because of the fury of
the oppressor."

He concluded his remarks with this challenge:[37]

Let's overcome cowardice with courage.
Let's be fearless ambassadors of Christ and
stand strong for the glory of God our Savior,
pulling others from the fire of eternal judge-
ment (Jude 23).

Standing for Righteousness

Franklin is not calling the pastors and evangelists of this
nation to do something he is not willing to do himself. He
has, in fact, become the model of a prophetic voice speaking
out boldly against the sins of our nation. In the process he has
taken the bull by the horns on many occasions. Consider his
comments on the following social and moral issues:

Abortion — "There is no place for compromise on straight-
forward issues such as abortion . . . God has given us
clear biblical direction that we must follow and obey . . .

As a minister of the Lord Jesus Christ, I believe this is a non-negotiable issue. Abortion is wrong. It is the murder of unborn children, and no law of the land and no party platform can ever legitimize it."[38]

Gun Control — "The gun control proposals now circulating in Washington and in many state capitals don't address a more important issue — the constant strain of violence put forth by the entertainment industry [in movies, music and video games]. But the problem — the real crux of the issue — lies not in the instruments of violence used . . . The root of violence is in the evil and depraved heart of man."[39]

Islam — "Islam is a religion of hatred. It's a religion of war."[40] "For Muslims, peace comes only through submission to Islam. When they speak of peace, they mean submission to their religion . . . Worldwide, tens of thousands of men, women and children have been slaughtered in the name of Allah, under the bloody flag of Islam."[41]

ISIS — "The evil of ISIS really shouldn't shock us — it is fully in keeping with their ultimate agenda of hastening a final apocalypse . . . One thing is for sure — one day every knee will bow and every tongue will confess that Jesus Christ is Lord, to the glory of God the Father."[42]

Hinduism — "No elephant with 100 arms can do anything for me. None of their 9,000 gods is going to lead me to salvation."[43]

Same-Sex Marriage — "True followers of Jesus Christ . . . cannot endorse same-sex marriage, regardless of what our President, the Congress, the Supreme Court, the media or the latest Gallup poll says about the matter . . . This moral issue has been settled by God Himself and is not subject to man-made revisions or modifications. In the end, I would rather be on the wrong side of public opinion than on the wrong side of Almighty God who established the standard of living for the world He created."[44]

Homosexuality — "The church is on dangerous ground when it departs from the teaching of Christ and attempts to redefine His commands and compromise His truth. There are many things in Scripture that Christians disagree on, but the Bible is crystal clear about the sanctity of life and marriage. It is also clear that homosexuality is spelled out as sin — there are no ifs, ands or buts."[45]

Transgender Restrooms — "[The idea] is not only ridiculous, it's unsafe. Common sense tells us that this would open the door, literally, to all sorts of serious concerns, including giving sexual predators access to children. It violates every sense of privacy and decency for people of both sexes, adults and children."[46]

Secularism — "When the Berlin Wall came down, everybody said we had won . . . [but then] Secularism came. And Secularism and Communism are the same thing. They're godless. They're anti-Christ."[47]

Christian Persecution — "Even in America there has recently grown an ugly, anti-Christian bias and intolerance that is changing our nation from the inside out, opening doors for all kinds of discrimination and loss of religious freedom that we hear about daily in the news."[48]

Government — "We're living now in a time where we see the spirit of the Antichrist at the government level."[49] "I have no confidence that any politician or any party is going to turn this country around. The only hope for this country is for men and women of God to take a stand."[50]

Fear — "Are we going to be cowards because we're afraid? Could we get our heads chopped off? We could, maybe one day. So what? Chop it off!"[51]

Taking on the President

On several occasions, Franklin boldly stood up to President Obama in public. In May of 2012 when Obama endorsed same-sex marriage, Graham denounced the President by declaring he had "shaken his fist at the same God who created and defined marriage."[52]

At the Presidential Prayer Breakfast in February of 2015, President Obama came across as defending Islamic acts of barbarity when he made the following observation: "Lest we get on our high horse and think this is unique to some other place, remember that during the Crusades and the Inquisition, people committed terrible deeds in the name of Christ."[53] Franklin's response was swift and powerful:[54]

> Mr. President, many people in history have used the name of Jesus Christ to accomplish evil things for their own desires. But Jesus taught peace, love and forgiveness. He came to give His life for the sins of mankind, not to take life. Muhammad, on the contrary, was a warrior and killed many innocent people. True followers of Christ emulate Christ — true followers of Muhammad emulate Muhammad.

Calling the Nation to Repentance

In 2015 Franklin announced that he planned to take his message of repentance to the entire nation during 2016 by holding prayer rallies in every state capital before the presidential election in November. He called it "The Decision America Tour."[55]

He said he was going to challenge Americans to:[56]

1) Pray earnestly for the nation.
2) Live out their faith boldly.
3) Take a stand for righteousness.

4) Run for public office.
5) Get out to vote.
6) Be salt and light for the nation.

Franklin Graham during his "Decision America" campaign.
(Photo courtesy of the Billy Graham Evangelistic Association)

Here's how Franklin summed up the overall purpose of the rallies:[57]

> The only hope for this country is Almighty God and His Son. We can't sit idly by any longer. LGBT activists, abortion rights advocates, aggressive atheist groups, and others who ignore God's Word are trying to shove their agenda down our throats. We need to take every opportunity to speak up for biblical standards and let our lights shine. We need to work to preserve our religious freedoms so that we can continue to proclaim the Gospel freely. If we as Christians stand together and let our voice be heard, I believe God can use us to make a difference. I hope you will start praying with us now.

Franklin's tour proved to be spectacularly successful. As he promised, he held prayer rallies in all 50 state capitals, beginning in Des Moines, Iowa in January 2016 and ending in Raleigh, North Carolina in October. A total of 236,950 people attended the rallies, an average of 5,000 per stop.[58] Over 8,000 people made professions of faith in Jesus as their Lord and Savior.[60]

He did not campaign for any political candidate. He campaigned for God. Over and over, he declared, "I have no hope in the Democratic Party, and I have no hope in the Republican Party. Zero hope."[60] Instead, he asserted, "Our only hope is God."[61]

Many explanations have been given for Donald Trump's surprising, amazing and even miraculous victory. I personally believe it was God's response to Franklin Graham's crusade, calling believers to repent, pray and vote.

Conclusion

We need to praise God for this courageous Christian leader. We need to pray for his safety. He is being reviled and persecuted more than any other Christian leader in America today.

And we who call ourselves Christians need to follow his example of standing for righteousness regardless of the consequences.

> *Be on your guard; stand firm in the faith; be courageous; be strong.* — 1 Corinthians 16:13 (NIV)

> *Blessed are those who have been persecuted for the sake of righteousness, for theirs is the kingdom of heaven.* — Matthew 5:10 (NASB)

Robert Jeffress

Chapter 12

Robert Jeffress:
A Voice Warning of
Impending Judgment

> *Now as for you, son of man, I have appointed*
> *you a watchman . . . so you will hear a mes-*
> *sage from My mouth and give them warning*
> *from Me.* — Ezekiel 33:7

Don Wildmon often bemoaned the fact that most pulpits in America are silent about our nation's moral problems — and that has certainly been true. But there have been exceptions over the years, like pastors Erwin Lutzer and David Jeremiah. Robert Jeffress, pastor of First Baptist Church in Dallas, Texas, is another one of the exceptions. He has never feared to tread — and tread boldly — where few pastors have been willing to go.

I often think of him as the "Harry Truman of American pastors" because, like President Truman, he spits words like bullets and seems to have no concern about who might be offended. To him, the truths of God's Word are more important than hurt feelings.

Taking a Stand for Righteousness

Jeffress came to national attention in 1998 while serving as the pastor of First Baptist Church in Wichita Falls, Texas. He was outraged when the city's library decided to provide two books about children with homosexual parents, trying to present such a family as "normal."When the library refused to remove the books, Jeffress checked them out, refused to return them, and paid a fine to cover the cost.[1] Like Don Wildmon's decision to call on people to turn off TV for a week, Jeffress' action caught the attention of the media, and overnight he was being featured in national newscasts.

In the following years Jeffress became known for his bold, biblical sermons dealing with hot-button moral issues like homosexual activity and abortion. In 2006 an organization called Vision America gave him their distinguished Daniel Award "for steadfast commitment and boldness in proclaiming the uncompromising Word of God."[2]

Communicating Effectively

PASTOR ROBERT JEFFRESS
FOX NEWS CONTRIBUTOR

Jeffress appears frequently on Fox News as a biblical commentator on national and international news events.
(www.outsidethebeltway.com)

One very interesting thing about Jeffress is that he understands how the media works, and he makes the most of it. Thus, whereas his more than 20 books contain very thoughtful, in-depth discussions of the moral issues afflicting our nation, when it comes to being interviewed on radio or television, Jeffress always speaks in short, savvy and colorful phrases. He does this because he knows that the broadcast media thrive on "sound bites."

Consider, for example, the sound bites he has delivered on the following topics:

- **Homosexuality** — "Gay is not okay. What homosexuals do is filthy. It is so degrading that it is beyond description. And it is their filthy behavior that explains why they are so much more prone to disease."[3]

- **Same-Sex Marriage** — "Such marriages are counterfeit."[4]

- **Islam** — "Islam is a false religion that will lead you to hell. It is based on a false book that is based on a fraud. It was founded by a false prophet who was leading people away instead of to the one true God."[5]

- **Judaism** — "The three greatest Jews in the New Testament — Peter, Paul and Jesus — all said Judaism won't do it, it's faith in Jesus Christ."[6]

- **Roman Catholicism** — "It is the Satanic result of Babylonian mystery religion."[7]

- **Mormonism** — "It is a heresy from the pit of Hell."[8]

- **Obama** — "President Obama is not the Antichrist. But what I am saying is this: the course he is choosing to lead our nation is paving the way for the future reign of the Antichrist."[9]

- **Spineless Pastors** — "Wimpy pastors produce wimpy Christians — and that is why we are losing this culture war."[10]

The Man

Who is this sharp-tongue prophetic spokesman and defender of the faith?

Robert Jeffress was born in 1955 in Dallas and grew up in First Baptist Church under the tutelage of its renowned pastor, Dr. W. A. Criswell. It's the church where he was baptized, married, ordained and preached his first Sunday sermon. It's also where he got his first job out of college as a youth pastor.[11]

At Criswell's memorial service in 2002, Jeffress said the pastor had taught him "to always work hard" and "to know the Bible as thoroughly as a doctor knows medicine and a lawyer knows law."[12] In an interview in 2012, Jeffress revealed that Criswell had once told him, "Robert, I want you to get to know every square inch of this church . . . because one day it will be yours."[13]

Jeffress got his undergraduate degree from Baylor University in Waco, Texas. He earned his seminary degree from Southwestern Baptist Theological Seminary in Ft. Worth, Texas. His graduate degrees, including his doctorate, were earned from Dallas Theological Seminary. He is married to his childhood sweetheart, Amy, and they are the parents of two daughters.[14]

Those who have testified about his childhood say that he was characterized by a sense of certitude from the moment he was born. He was always certain about God, the Bible, Jesus and his salvation. He seemed never to have any doubts.[15] His sister once said, "It's like he came into this world as a little adult."[16]

His first pastorate was in East Texas. In 1992 he became pastor of First Baptist Church in Wichita Falls, Texas where he served for 15 years. Criswell's prophecy concerning Jeffress was fulfilled in 2007 when he was called to become the pastor of First Baptist Church in Dallas. At the time, the church was in decline, but Jeffress quickly revitalized it with his passionate biblical preaching, his controversial stands for moral righteousness, and a highly imaginative and bold $128 million replacement of most of the church's facilities.

Jeffress was featured on the cover of *D Magazine* in January 2012. (www.dmagazine.com)

Jeffress began speaking prophetically about our nation in 2012 with the publication of his book, *Twilight's Last Gleaming*.[17] In 2013 he was invited to be the keynote speaker at the annual Bible conference sponsored by Lamb & Lion Ministries. At that conference, he presented a condensed version of the thesis of his book. An edited version is presented below.[18]

The Implosion of America

Robert Jeffress

I believe America's collapse is inevitable.

I came to understand why this is true just a couple years ago when we were in the midst of preparing for the building of our new church campus. We had to first of all get rid of five of our buildings, consisting of about 600,000 square feet in the middle of downtown Dallas. And so the question arose: How do you get rid of that many buildings in the middle of downtown Dallas without bringing down the surrounding skyscrapers?

The demolition people met with me, and they said the best way to achieve this is through an implosion. And they explained to me what they were going to do. They said, "We're going to take 200 pounds of dynamite and attach it to key structural supports within those five buildings. We will then explode the dynamite, there will be a pause, and then the law of physics will take over. Without those foundational supports, the buildings will fall in on themselves under their own weight." I said, "Well, that sounds pretty good to me. Let's do it."

And so, on a brisk October morning in 2010, they closed downtown Dallas. The Mayor and I and our building committee chairman were on a nearby roof top, along with all of the media. CNN, Fox News, and all the local media were there to cover the implosion of our buildings. This was going out live on Fox and Friends and other media outlets around the world.

We did the countdown, 5-4-3-2-1. The Mayor and I pressed the ceremonial red button, and in the next block we heard the explosions going off just like they predicted. And those explosions were followed by nothing. Absolutely nothing! I cannot begin to tell you what all went through my mind over those next few seconds. I began to think, "Who am I going to fire first?" I could just see this scene being replayed endlessly on YouTube, "Pastor's Implosion a Dud." I mean it seemed like forever. But you see, I had forgotten what the demolition people told me. They had told me there was going to be a pause after those explosions.

And suddenly, without any warning, I heard a sound that could only be compared to standing in front of a jet engine. The roar increased in volume as we watched those once mighty buildings fall in on themselves, and within 30 seconds, they were reduced to nothing more than a plume of debris-filled dust.

I learned something that morning about implosions. They begin with a series of seemingly unrelated explosions, followed by a pause, and then a sudden collapse.

Four Explosive Decisions

Ladies and gentlemen, over the last 50 years our Supreme Court has made four explosive decisions that have so weakened the moral and spiritual structure and foundation of our country that our inevitable collapse is certain. Right now we're simply living between that time of the explosions that have weakened our basic foundation, and the coming implosion.

These four decisions have changed the direction of our country more than any congressional mandate and more than any executive order from the President of the United States. What are those four decisions?

Explosion Number One

Decision number one — I call it explosion number one — was the Supreme Court case in 1962 of *Engel v. Vitale.* This is the case that removed the saying of a prayer in the public schools.

A simple 22-word voluntary prayer was deemed unconstitutional. And of course, it is from that decision that all of the other court decisions cascaded concerning prayer, showing government is not neutral toward religion, but rather is hostile toward it. And government is especially hostile toward the Christian religion.

Explosion Number Two

From that decision eventually came the decision in 1980 of *Stone v. Graham* which stopped the posting of the Ten Commandments in public schools. Specifically, that case came out of the public schools of Kentucky where copies of the Ten Commandments were posted on the school walls.

And what was the Court's reasoning for removing the Ten Commandments from our schools? If I were to paraphrase this for you, you would think I was making it up. So I want to read to you the Supreme Court's decision and their reasoning for removing the posting of the Ten Commandments. The Court said:

> If the posted copies of the Ten Commandments are to have any effect at all, it will induce the school children to read, meditate upon, perhaps venerate and obey the Commandments. This is not a permissible state objective under the establishment clause of the First Amendment.

In other words, if we post the Ten Commandments, children may actually read, venerate and, heaven forbid, obey them!

Now, even if the Supreme Court had ruled correctly, that doesn't change God's law. You see, God's law never changes. But the fact is the Supreme Court did not rule correctly. Consider this — 118 years earlier the Supreme Court had said in the case of Vidal v. Girard's Executors:

> Why may not the Bible, especially the New Testament without note or comment be read and taught as a divine revelation in the [schools] — its general precepts expounded, its evidences explained, and its glorious principle of morality inculcated? Where can the purest principles of morality be learned so clearly, or so perfectly as from the New Testament?

The Meaning of the First Amendment

Now you have to ask yourself the question, "What's

changed?" The Constitution hasn't changed. What has changed is our culture. We have allowed the liberal activists to pervert the meaning of the First Amendment. Let's be clear about what the First Amendment says and what it doesn't say.

The First Amendment, commonly known as the establishment clause, says, "Congress shall make no law respecting an establishment of religion, or prohibiting the free exercise thereof." That Amendment simply says Congress cannot establish a state church and it cannot prohibit the free exercise of religion. And yet we have people who have perverted that into meaning that there is some imaginary freedom *from* religion that is found in the Constitution.

Did you notice here in our metroplex, just a couple of weeks ago, that a Joshua High School student who was valedictorian of his class dared to violate the school's regulation and mentioned Jesus Christ in his speech? He was threatened with having his career at the Naval Academy ruined because he did such a thing! And the public school district lawyer said this: "We have to balance this student's right and freedom of religion with other students' freedom from religion."

Where is that in the Constitution? There is no constitutional guarantee that somebody doesn't have to listen to a prayer at a graduation ceremony or see a nativity in the public square, or look at the Ten Commandments in the courthouse. That is nowhere in the Constitution. What the Constitution says is everyone is free to practice his or her religion.

Explosion Number Three

Explosive decision number three was rooted right here in the Dallas-Ft. Worth Metroplex. It was the 1973 decision in the case of *Roe vs. Wade*. It is the decision that has resulted now in the murder of over 50 million children in the womb.

By the way, whenever I am on television talking about this, I never allow the phrase to be used, "a woman's right to choose" without completing the sentence: "It is a woman's right to choose to murder her child." Don't let anybody else get by without completing that full sentence. That's what this is about. And that is what *Roe vs. Wade* has done. It has sanctioned the killing of unborn children . . .

In my book, *Twilight's Last Gleaming*, I cited a study that says that if the 50 million children who have been killed in the last 50 years had been allowed to live and grow up and become productive citizens, they would have added anywhere from 35 to 70 trillion dollars to our gross national product. If those 50 million children had been allowed to grow up and live and contribute to society, there would be no Social Security crisis. There would be no Medicare crisis. They would have been paying into the system. You cannot slaughter 20% of your population, no nation can, without severe economic repercussions.

Ladies and gentlemen, the economic repercussions of abortion pale in significance to the most heinous and disastrous result of abortion, and that is the certainty of God's judgment. All you have to do is look at history and see how God has dealt with nations that kill their children. In the Old Testament God raised up the Assyrians and the Babylonians to judge Israel for participating in child sacrifice. During the Second World War God raised up the allied forces to crush Nazi Germany for taking children to the gas chambers by the train loads.

Looking at history, does anybody have to wonder how God is going to deal with a nation like ours that sanctions the killing of children? . . .

Explosion Number Four

The fourth explosive decision was *Lawrence and Garner vs. the State of Texas* in 2003. This is the Supreme Court decision that struck down our state's anti-sodomy laws. It was the beginning of a domino effect that we see continuing today.

What is interesting is in that decision in 2003 Justice Scalia at that time said, "This reasoning leaves on pretty shaky ground the state laws limiting marriage to opposite-sex couples." Justice Scalia was being prophetic. In fact it was the reasoning of that court in 2003 that led to the recent decision that struck down a part of the Defense of Marriage Act.

What you need to understand is that for 226 years our judiciary has understood that the relationship between a man and woman is what constitutes marriage, and it is the bedrock of social order. James Kent, who served as Chief Justice of the [New York] Supreme Court, wrote in his commentary on American Law:

> The primary and most important of the domestic relations is that of husband and wife. It has its foundation in nature and is the only relation by which Providence has permitted the continuance of the human race . . .

What we saw in the recent DOMA decision is the Supreme Court caving in to political correctness. Now you know, people say — even Christians — "Well so what? What harm is it to me that homosexuals want to get married? How does that hurt me?" Well, first of all it's not all about you and me, it is about society. But the fact is it does harm society.

The Hoover Institute has done long-term studies on Scandinavian countries that legalized same-sex marriage. Do you know what they found? They found that in countries that legalize same-sex marriage the rate of heterosexual marriage drops precipitously. And the reason is obvious: If marriage becomes anything you want it to be, why bother to get married at all? It was reported last week that our marriage rate here in the United States has dropped to the lowest level it has been in a century. And so you create tremendous instability in society when you allow that to happen . . .

God knew what He was doing when He designed the family. And ladies and gentlemen, even though Supreme Court opinions change, even though culture changes, God's Word never changes. He is the one who designed marriage and He knows how it best operates.

Now my point in citing these four cases is simply this: no nation that outlaws the acknowledgment of God in the public square, that sanctions the killing of unborn children and destroys the most basic unit of society, the family — no such nation can survive. The explosions have already occurred. The implosion is coming. We are simply living in the in-between-time.

The Christian Response

Now the question is, "How are we as Christians to respond to all this?" I want to suggest to you that we turn to the words of our Lord and Savior Jesus Christ who told us exactly how we are to respond to a decaying culture. In Matthew 5:13 Jesus said:

> You are the salt of the earth, but if the salt has become tasteless how will it be made salty again? It is good for nothing anymore except to be thrown out and trampled underfoot by men.

Advertising banner for Jeffress' television program.
(https://ptv.org/)

Jesus said our first responsibility as believers is to act as salt. Do you know that in Jesus' day salt was a preservative? In the day before refrigerators, salt was the way to delay the decay of the meat. What salt did was simply give the meat a little longer shelf life. Eventually the meat would rot and would have to be discarded. The salt delayed that process . .

What I believe Jesus is saying to us is, "We're not going to prevent the destruction of America, but we can delay it so we have more opportunity to share the Gospel." I therefore believe God has called us as Christians to stand up and push back against the tide of evil and immorality that is sweeping our country.

A Call for Christian Courage

I tell you, I am sick and tired of these wimpy Christians who mask their timidity and lack of courage with some sort of pseudo-spirituality that says, "Well, you know, we're just not citizens of this world, we are citizens of Heaven. And you know, we just need to let the world take its course."

Look, God never encouraged us to engage in silo-spirituality — to separate our faith from the rest of what's happening in this world. The fact is there are a lot of people in your church right now, perhaps even your pastor, who think for a Christian to use his faith to try to influence other people or unbelievers, or the course of this nation, well that's un-American, un-Christian and it may be illegal.

Listen, Jesus Christ is not just Lord of the Church, He is Lord over all creation. Jesus isn't just interested in religious people and religious institutions, Jesus is interested in every institution, and He's interested in government as well. Whenever you say that God doesn't want us to influence our culture, just start looking at the Bible itself. Look at men of God like Jonah, and David, and Jeremiah, and Isaiah, and in the New Testament, men like John the Baptist.

When you look at the ministries of those men, you will see that they didn't just preach to themselves. Nor did they just preach to God's own people. These men of God were willing to stand up in an ungodly culture and confront ungodly leaders and say without stuttering or stammering, "Thus saith the Lord." We need men of God like that today to do the same. We need men of God who will stand up and say compassionately yet courageously, "Abortion is murder." "Homosexuality is a perversion of God's plan for human sexuality." And "God will reject any nation that rejects Him."

You know, when you say that Christians shouldn't try to influence society, you are completely negating Jesus' words when He said, "You are the salt of the earth." How do we influence the world? How do we push back against immorality? It is by engaging in that dirty, filthy word called politics.

Now you know I hear this all the time: "Christians shouldn't get involved in politics." Do you know what the word politics means? The word means to influence, to control. When you say Christians shouldn't get involved in politics what you are saying is that Christians shouldn't try to influence the society in which they live. Can anybody say that with a straight face and believe it?

Christians and Politics

Let me ask you three questions: Do you believe that God cares about 50 million children being murdered in the womb? Do you think God has any opinion about that? Do you think that God cares about the rampant immorality that is sweeping our land? Do you think that God cares at all about His name being outlawed from mention in the public square? If you've answered yes, you have just explained why Christians ought to be involved in politics.

You see, in the Old Testament times it was the king who determined the spiritual direction of the nation. If he was a righteous king, God blessed the nation. If he was an unrighteous king, God cursed the nation. But as John Jay, the first Chief Justice of the Supreme Court, said, "God has given us the privilege of selecting our leaders. And it is the duty and preference of Christians to prefer and select Christians as their leaders."

Every time I use that quote the liberals go crazy, but those were the words of the first Chief Justice of the Supreme Court. It is our duty to prefer and select Christians as our leaders. Every time you go into the voting booth, you are either casting a vote for righteousness or for unrighteousness. And if we're going to push back against this evil we have to get involved — not to save America because we are not going to save America. But we can delay our nation's collapse if we get involved.

Why Push Back?

The reason we want to buy more time for America is so we as Christians can fulfill our ultimate calling as believers, as stated by Jesus in Matthew 5:14 — "You are the light of the world."

Listen, God has not called us to save America. God has called us to save Americans from the coming judgment of God. The only way that can happen is by introducing them to a personal faith in the Lord Jesus Christ. The reason we want to buy time for our culture is so that we have the opportunity to do just that . . .

A Fundamental Principle About Light

You know why Paul said we could rejoice in the culture in which we are living, even though it may be very wicked? He understood a very simple principle — the darker the background, the brighter the light.

I experienced an illustration of that not long ago. I was helping my younger daughter celebrate a special occasion in her life. I said, "Dorothy, I'll take you to the mall and get you anything you want." Now when I said, "anything you want," I had in mind going to a shop like Forever 21 and getting a $20 or $30 dress. So, we go over to North Park Shopping Center and she leads me right past Forever 21 and right into a jewelry store! We're standing there in front of the counter, and the salesman approaches, looks at my daughter and says, "Good to see you again." At that moment, I knew I'd been had! He said, "Would you like to look at that ring you were looking at yesterday?" She said, "Yes."

So he went back and brought forth a little tray with different rings on it and picked out the one she had been looking at. Before he sat it down on the plexiglass counter he took a piece of black velvet, spread it out on the counter and then took that ring and plopped it right in the center of the black velvet. The contrast between that black velvet and the light emitting from the ring was so stark it almost blinded me to the price, not quite, but it almost did. You see, that salesman understood a fundamental principle: the darker the background, the brighter the light.

The Opportunity Provided by Darkness

Listen, we are living in dark days today, no doubt about it. But the more hopeless this world becomes the brighter the hope of Jesus Christ shines.

So which is it? Are we to be salt? Are we to get involved in politics and try to push back against evil? Or, are we to be light involved in evangelism and sharing the Gospel? It's not an either-or answer. It is both-and. God has called us to do both. He has called us to be balanced. But please don't equate that word balanced with passive. This is not time for Christians living in America to be passive.

I'm reminded of the words of William Watkins in his book, *The New Absolutes*. He wrote:

> As Christians we must reject the new tolerance and become a people marked by intolerance. Not an intolerance that unleashes hate upon people. But an intolerance that is unwilling to allow error to masquerade as truth any longer. An intolerance that is willing to stand up and call evil, evil and good, good.

May God grant us the courage to do just that.

An Additional Explosion

Since this speech was delivered in 2013, the Supreme Court of the United States has set off an additional explosion — its abominable decision in June 2015 to legalize same-sex marriage, making our nation's implosion even more certain and more imminent.

It was a despicable day in American history when President Obama decided to celebrate this court decision by lighting up the White House in the colors of the Sexual Perversion Movement.

A Great Opportunity

In January of 2017 Jeffress was granted the high honor of being invited to deliver the inauguration sermon to President-elect Trump and his family and staff at St. John's Episcopal Church, located across the street from the White House.

The sermon was short and to the point. Jeffress focused on the story of Nehemiah rebuilding the walls of Jerusalem, and he commented wryly at the beginning, "You see, God is *not* against wall building."[19] Jeffress emphasized three points in his sermon. First, he assured Trump that he would face major criticisms as any "true leader" does because there are only three ways to avoid criticism: "do nothing, say nothing and be nothing." He encouraged Trump to not allow his critics to distract him.[20]

Second, Jeffress stressed that Nehemiah refused to allow setbacks to stop him. As with criticism, Jeffress assured Trump he would suffer many setbacks, and he encouraged him not to allow them to discourage or stop him.[21]

Third, Jeffress underlined the fact that Nehemiah sought God's help to empower him. In like manner, Jeffress told Trump that he would never be able to accomplish his goals in his own power or with his own natural abilities. Rather, he would "need God's supernatural power."[22]

Jeffress concluded his sermon by reminding Trump of two quotations — one from Ronald Reagan and the other from the Bible. The Reagan quote was taken from a speech of his to the Republican National Convention in Dallas in 1984. He said: "America needs God more than God needs America. If we ever forget that we are 'one nation under God,' then we will be a nation gone under."

The Scripture quote was taken from Psalm 33:12:

Blessed is the nation whose God is the LORD.

Jonathan Cahn

Chapter 13

Jonathan Cahn: A Voice Declaring Impending Destruction

While they are saying, "Peace and safety!"
then destruction will come upon them sud-
denly like labor pains upon a woman with
child, and they will not escape. —

1 Thessalonians 5:3

Jonathan David Cahn burst onto the national scene with a big bang in 2011 with the publication of his blockbuster, best-selling novel, *The Harbinger*.[1] It was a well written and highly imaginative work of fiction which contained a much-needed, biblically-based and ominous message for the America people.

The thesis of the book was that our nation has turned its back on God and that the 9/11 attacks were a remedial judgment calling us to repentance. Further, if we ignore this call, God will move us from judgment to destruction.

The book revolves around a passage in Isaiah 9:10 which reads as follows:

> The bricks have fallen down,
> But we will rebuild with smooth stones;
> The sycamores have been cut down,
> But we will replace them with cedars.

Many, including Cahn, have referred to this verse as a prophecy, but it is not. Instead, it is a descriptive verse that tells how Israel responded to a national calamity when it was invaded by the Assyrians in 732 BC. Instead of recognizing the invasion as a remedial judgment and repenting, the Jewish people responded in pride, vowing to build back bigger and better than ever.

Cahn refers to this verse about half the time as a vow, which it is, but the rest of the time he calls it a "prophecy for Israel and a sign for America."[2] Admittedly, this gets a little confusing at times, but it is not something to get lathered up about.

The point Cahn makes, which is unassailable, is that our nation responded to the 9/11 attacks with the same attitude as ancient Israel — one of defiance rather than repentance. Instead of falling on our knees and repenting of our rebellion against God and His Word, we engaged in a national orgy of patriotism. "God Bless America" bumper stickers appeared everywhere, and our political leaders began to brag about how we would rebuild bigger and better. They even began to quote Isaiah 9:10 in their speeches!

Cahn's highlighting of this verse in his book was right on target and was much needed. Since that time, it has become obvious that instead of repenting, most Americans reacted like a sleepy man who responds to his alarm clock by hitting the snooze button and then turning over and going back to sleep.

But Jonathan Cahn has continued to cry out from the depths of his heart, like the Old Testament prophets did as they warned of impending judgments and ultimate destruction.

The Man

Who's this charismatic man who writes with such imagination and speaks with such fervor?

Jonathan Cahn was born in Englewood, New Jersey in 1959 and grew up in Nanuet, New York, a suburb of New York City. His mother's parents escaped persecution in Russia and ended up in Brooklyn where his mother was born. His father escaped Nazi Germany, and after periods of time in England and Canada, he moved to the United States. His parents met each other while pursuing their doctorates in chemistry.[3]

Cahn was raised in a Reformed Jewish household. He attended synagogue regularly, but he became an atheist when he was eight years old. He later abandoned atheism, but he continued to question Judaism, and so he refused to partake in the ususal Bar Mitzvah ceremonies that mark a young boy's transition into manhood.[4]

When he was in the seventh grade, he was confronted by a classmate who told him about Jesus. This prompted him to start investigating the meaning of life. He began to read about the supernatural, the occult, the paranormal, UFOs, Nostradamus, religion and philosophy. One day he saw a book that he mistakenly thought was about UFOs. It was titled *The Late Great Planet Earth*. The book was a turning point for him because it drove him into the Scriptures, and he began to discover Bible prophecies about the Messiah that had been fulfilled in the life of Jesus.[5]

Cahn attended The State University of New York at Purchase where he majored in history. After two very serious auto accidents in which he had close calls with death, Cahn decided at age 20 to receive Jesus as his Lord and Savior.[6] Soon thereafter, he started teaching a Bible study. After graduation, he went to work for a homeless outreach charity that provided food and counseling for people living on the streets of New York City.[7]

In 1988, he was invited to become the spiritual leader of a small, 35 member, Messianic congregation in Garfield,

New Jersey, called Beth Israel. The congregation began to grow rapidly under his leadership, and in 2008, it moved to Wayne, New Jersey, which is located less than 20 miles from midtown Manhattan. Today, it is the largest Messianic congregation in America.[8]

Cahn has a second ministry called "Hope of the World." This is an international outreach of teaching, evangelism and compassion projects for the needy.[9]

The Book

The Harbinger is the story of a journalist who is confronted by a mysterious man whom he calls "the prophet." This man appears and then disappears repeatedly throughout the book. Each time he appears, he gives the journalist a clue about the spiritual meaning of the 9/11 attacks.

As he does so, he opens the eyes of the journalist to spiritual parallels between the Assyrian attack on ancient Israel in 732 BC and the attacks on the World Trade Towers and the Pentagon in 2001. He emphasizes that both Israel and America were blessed beyond anything experienced by any other nation in history. And yet, both ultimately drifted from God. Here's how the prophet in Cahn's book describes it:[10]

> It started with a spiritual complacency, then spiritual confusion, then the merging of God with idols, and then ultimately, the rejection of His ways. Just as with ancient Israel, America began ruling God out of its life, turning, step by step, against His ways, at first

subtly, and then more and more brazenly.

This analysis prompted the journalist to ask the prophet when all this rejection of God began in the United States. The prophet responded:[11]

> In the middle of the twentieth century, America began officially removing God from its national life. It abolished prayer and Scripture in its public schools. As ancient Israel had removed the Ten Commandments from its national consciousness, so America did likewise, removing the Ten Commandments from public view, banning it from its public squares, and taking it down, by government decree, from its walls.

> As it was in ancient Israel, so too in America, God was progressively driven out of the nation's public life. The very mention of the name *God* or *Jesus* in any relevant context became more and more taboo and unwelcome unless for the purpose of mockery and attack. That which had once been revered as sacred was now increasingly treated as profanity. And as God was driven out, idols were brought in to replace Him.

When the prophet mentioned idols, the journalist protested that Americans were not so primitive as to worship idols. The prophet assured him that idols had replaced God in American life — "They just don't call them *idols.*" He continued:[12]

> As God was expunged from American life, idols came in to fill the void — idols of sensuality, idols of greed, of money, success, comfort, materialism, pleasure, sexual immorality, self-worship, self-obsession. The sacred

increasingly disappeared, and the profane took its place. It was another kind of spiritual amnesia: the nation forgot its foundations, its purpose, and its calling.

The standards and values it had long upheld were now abandoned. What it had once known as immoral, it now accepted. Its culture was increasingly corrupted by the corrosion of sexual immorality, growing continuously more crude and vulgar. A wave of pornography began penetrating its media. The same nation that had once been dedicated to spreading God's light to the nations now filled the world with the pornographic and the obscene.

The journalist once again tried to defend our nation by arguing that we are not as bad as ancient Israel. He reminded the prophet that Israel became so deranged as a nation that they offered their children as sacrifices to pagan gods. The prophet immediately reminded him that ten years after removing prayer and Bible reading from the public schools, our Supreme Court legalized the killing of the unborn:[13]

The blood of the innocent now stained its collective hands. Israel had sacrificed thousand on the altars of Baal and Molech. But by the dawn of the twenty-first century, America had sacrificed *millions.*

The prophet declared that America's hedge of protection has been removed, and the nation is in danger of judgment.[14] Again and again, the prophet emphasized that instead of responding to 9/11 with repentance, the nation brazenly resumed "its departure from God and its rejection of His ways, only now with increased speed."[15] And over and over, the prophet stressed that the only hope of America was to return to God.

An Incredible Revelation

The most fascinating aspect of the book is contained in a chapter titled, "Mystery Ground."[16] The prophet reminds the journalist that the original capital of our nation was New York City. And when George Washington was sworn in as our nation's first president on April 30, 1789, that ceremony took place in Federal Hall in New York.

After Washington finished delivering his inaugural address, he led the nation's first government on foot to St. Paul's Chapel where he and all the Senators and Representatives bowed together in prayer to consecrate the new nation's future into the hands of God.

Jonathan Cahn is shown above standing across the Hudson River from New York City, with "Ground Zero" in the background.
(www.christianpost.com)

And where is St. Paul's Chapel? At "Ground Zero" where the attacks occurred on the World Trade Towers. St. Paul's Chapel was the only building in the vicinity that was not destroyed or seriously damaged! The prophet refers to the site as "America's ground of consecration."[17] And he proceeds to point out: "It was here that they came to commit the nation's future to God's holy protection. And it was here where that holy protection would be withdrawn."[18]

It was at this point that the prophet reminded the journalist of some words from Washington's inaugural address concerning the providence of God:[19]

> No people can be bound to acknowledge and adore the Invisible Hand which conducts the affairs of men more than those of the United States. Every step by which they have advanced to the character of an independent nation seems to have been distinguished by some token of providential agency.

The prophet concluded his remarks about Washington by pointing out that he had uttered a prophecy in his inaugural address: "The propitious smiles of Heaven can never be expected on a nation that disregards the eternal rules of order and right which Heaven itself hath ordained."[20]

It was a clear warning that the day America turns away from God will be the day that God starts removing His blessings from the nation.

Subsequent Presentations

Cahn was invited to present his message in January of 2013 at the Presidential Inaugural Prayer Breakfast in Washington, D.C. Unfortunately, the re-elected President Barack Obama did not attend. It was at this inaugural that President Obama would become the first President in history to call for the advancement of homosexual rights in an inaugural address.

As in his book, Cahn focused on comparing modern day America with ancient Israel. He emphasized the many parallels between the two — first the incredible blessings, then the turning away from God, followed by prophetic warnings and remedial judgments. And just as God finally delivered Israel over to destruction, Cahn warned that America is on the verge of suffering the same fate.[21]

Cahn painted a vivid and heartbreaking picture of our nation's rebellion against the very One who had showered us with blessings:[22]

> The nation that was established to bring the Word and light of God to the world, now fills the earth with pornography. We too now call evil "good" and good "evil." And what we once knew to be immoral, we now celebrate, and what we once knew to be right, we now war against. American culture has become turned in upon itself, a civilization at war against the very foundation on which it has been established . . .

> It is a new America in which one can be banned from the public square simply for believing the Bible, where profanity is treated as holy and the Holy as profane, a new America where the Bible is treated as contraband and nativity scenes are seen as dangerous.

> Our culture has grown increasingly vulgar, godless, and darkened. We too now defile, ridicule, and blaspheme the name of God. It wasn't too long ago that American television closed its broadcasting days with sermons. Now, our televisions and computer screens are filled with words and images once unimaginable, and God and Jesus have now become objects of comedy and mockery.

> It's as if a spiritual amnesia has overtaken the land. The Lord asked Israel, "Can a nation forget its God?" And yet Israel forgot. And now we too have forgotten. America has for-

gotten her God . . .

> The "city on a hill" has grown dark. Its lamp has grown dim. Its glory is fading. For God is not mocked. No nation can war against the very source of its blessings and expect those blessings to remain.

Cahn concluded this powerful address with this warning:[23]

> The time is late. The hour is critical. A great nation proceeds in rapid descent. And the signs of warning and judgment are manifesting in the land. The shadow of judgment is upon us.

In January of 2017, Cahn was invited to return and speak once again to the inaugural prayer breakfast. He began this address by noting that John Winthrop (1587-1649), one of our nation's founders, delivered a vision of the new nation in a sermon that he preached as he sailed to the new world in 1630 on a ship called the *Arbella*. If our nation followed the ways of God, he declared, then "The Lord . . . will command a blessing upon us in all our ways . . . He shall make us a praise and glory . . . For we must consider that we shall be as a city upon a hill."[24]

Cahn then proceeded to demonstrate that the "shining city upon a hill" has become a darkened slum whose light has gone out. He denounced our "idols of carnality and gain" and our "gods of materialism and licentiousness."[25] He condemned our killing of the unborn, stating that "we have descended to the darkest of sins."[26]

He refused to blame all the nation's sins upon President Obama. Rather, he stated that "a nation's apostasy cannot be blamed on any one leader. It is the nation that is ultimately accountable."[27] Yet, he hastened to declare that "in the past eight years America's spiritual fall and moral descent has both deepened and accelerated."[28]

He then outlined what he had in mind:[29]

- The present administration has led this nation to champion the killing of the unborn . . .

- The present administration has labored to strike down the standards and order ordained by God concerning man and woman and marriage . . .

- Under the present administration, relations between the United States and Israel have been brought to their lowest point in the history of the two nations.

- Under the present administration, the government has used the powers of state to force believers to commit acts against the commandments of God, to take part in the overturning and destruction of God's sacred order of marriage . . .

- And for the first time in American history, those who refused to violate the Word of God faced being put in prison by the state.

He next turned his attack to the presidential campaign of the past year, and he noted that for the first time in American history, a major presidential candidate — namely, Hillary Clinton — uttered these words: "Deep seated religious beliefs . . . must be changed." Cahn called this a declaration of war against God.[30]

Commenting on the outcome of the election, Cahn emphasized how totally unexpected it was. He characterized the victory of Donald Trump as "a window of mercy."[31] But

The author interviewing Cahn on Lamb & Lion's television program,
"Christ in Prophecy."

he made it clear that America's future did not depend on Trump: "The only way America will be great again is for America to return to the God who made America great in the first place."[32]

He concluded with a "charge to the new President:"[33]

> Your authority comes not from man but from God, the King above all kings. Therefore, submit your life to His authority and by His authority you shall lead.

> Do justly. Love mercy, and walk humbly with your God.

> Your life has been a vessel of your will. Now it must become the vessel of *His* will and *His* purposes.

> Uphold His ways, and you shall be upheld. Keep His Word and you shall be kept. Give honor to His name, above all names, and *your* name shall be honored.

The Response

People love pillow prophets. They hate true prophets. Pillow prophets tell people what they want to hear. They cry, "Peace and safety!" when danger is imminent. True prophets warn of danger and cry for repentance.

When Jeremiah told the people of Judah that it was God's will for them to surrender to the Babylonians and go into captivity, he was demonized as a false prophet and a traitor, and the people tried to kill him.

In like manner, Jonathan Cahn has been the victim of irresponsible and vicious attacks. He has been accused of "parading as a prophet." Others have branded him a "false prophet." These charges are reckless, unwarranted and un-Christ-like. Jonathan Cahn's message is thoroughly biblical. It is not based on any new revelation from God. Rather, it is based on the biblical principles that govern God's relationship with nations.

False Prophet?

The charge that he is a "false prophet" is downright ludicrous. His message is that America is in rebellion against God, that God has placed remedial judgments upon us, and that if we do not repent, God will deliver us from judgment to destruction. I ask you, "What part of that message is unbiblical?"

Furthermore, the Bible defines a false prophet as one who prophesies events that do not come to pass. If Rabbi Cahn prophesied that a specific event would take place on a specific date and that date were to come and go without the event happening, then he could legitimately be labeled as a "false prophet." But he has done no such thing.

He is simply declaring biblical principles. He is reminding us of the following truths:

- That when a richly blessed nation like ours sets its face against God, the judgment of God will fall upon it.

- That the only way for a rebellious nation to avoid the ultimate judgment of God — namely, destruction — is for it to repent.

Misuse of Scripture?

Others have attacked Rabbi Cahn because they argue that he has taken a scripture directed to ancient Israel (Isaiah 9:10) and has applied it to the United States. Again, I ask, "What is wrong with that?" If the scripture is applicable, why not apply it to our nation?

Actually, we do that all the time. The Psalms and Proverbs were written to the Jewish people, yet we apply them to ourselves. Should we reject the 23rd Psalm because it was not specifically addressed to the Church?

Incredibly, Rabbi Cahn has been criticized for applying 2 Chronicles 7:14 to the United States. It reads as follows:

> [If] My people who are called by My name humble themselves and pray and seek My face and turn from their wicked ways, then I will hear from heaven, will forgive their sin and will heal their land.

Are we actually going to contend that this scripture applies only to Israel? Are we really going to argue that if the professing Christians of this nation were to sincerely repent of their sins and the sins of our nation, that God would ignore it?

This particular scripture contains a timeless principle about repentance that even applies to pagan nations. Thus, when God sent the prophet Jonah to the pagan city of Nineveh with a message of "Turn or Burn!" the Lord changed His mind when the king put on sack cloth and ashes, repented, and called for the whole city to do likewise.

Or consider the seven letters contained in the second and third chapters of Revelation. Each one was addressed to a specific church located in the area of Asia Minor (modern day Turkey). Do the letters apply only to those specific churches? Of course not! They are just as relevant to the Church at large today as they were when they were written to the seven specific churches in the First Century.

Jumping to Conclusions

Many of the criticisms of Rabbi Cahn's message are based on unwarranted conclusions that people have jumped to in an effort to find something to criticize. For example, he has been accused of teaching that America is in a covenant relationship with God. The fact of the matter is that he has never said that. He simply notes that America's founding fathers believed that, and therefore they consecrated the nation to God.

Another unwarranted conclusion is that he teaches Isaiah 9:10 was a prophecy about the United States rather than Israel. Again, Rabbi Cahn has never made such an assertion. What he teaches instead is that the ancient pattern of judgment that occurred in Israel is now recurring in America, and in "a stunningly precise way."

A Book and a Sermon

Christians should be giving Rabbi Cahn a standing ovation, and many have. But some leaders of discernment ministries have tried, instead, to crucify him.

I know a genuine prophetic voice when I hear one. Cahn is the successor to David Wilkerson who began delivering the same message in the 1970's.

The current unbridled, petty and vicious attacks on Rabbi Cahn smack of what I would call "Christian McCarthyism." There are hyper-critics within Christianity today who are yelling "Apostate! Apostate!" over matters that really amount to nothing. If a person speaks to a group they disapprove of, they label him an "Apostate." If he has a different viewpoint from theirs about a non-essential doctrine, he is branded an "Apostate." If he compliments someone they don't like, he is relegated to Hell as an "Apostate."

An Appeal for Sanity

Grant Phillips, a Bible teacher in Kentucky who has pastored six churches in his lifetime, recently responded to the hysterical critics of Jonathan Cahn with these words:[34]

> Look folks, many of us need to . . . stop nit-picking everything the Lord is trying to tell us and just listen to what He is saying in whatever manner He chooses to say it. Even in my own experience of writing articles, every now and then, someone emails me who just wants to nit-pick at something I wrote while missing the message of the article. The phrase comes to mind, "They're so heavenly minded, they're no earthly good." We need to humble our hearts and stop being so self-righteous.

In my personal correspondence with Jonathan Cahn, I have discovered that he has a very Christ-like spirit and a great sense of humor. In responding to his critics, he has killed them with kindness, refusing to respond with the same invective they have used in attacking him. He has dealt with issues and not personalities.

And his sense of humor has helped him to put the criticism in perspective. Let me give you some examples:

- In response to crazy allegations that he is some-how involved in advocating the prosperity message of the Word of Faith Movement, he wrote: "I not only speak against those doctrines regularly, but my author's photo was taken at Sears Budget Photo!"

- In response to a looney assertion that he is advocating Replacement Theology, he wrote: "I'm Jewish and a believer. In order to subscribe to Replacement Theology, I'd have to replace myself with myself. I'm open to trying, but it just strikes me as a lot of work to end up no better off than when I started!"

- In response to the nutty charge that he is espousing principles of Mormonism, he wrote: "Okay, I was once into Donny and Marie Osmond, but when they started singing 'I'm a Little Bit Country, and I'm a Little Bit Rock and Roll,' I drew the line. You see, I don't believe in mixing doctrines."

- In response to the absurd allegation that he is involved in some way in Masonry, he replied: "It's true. I once had involvement with Masonry. It happened when I appeared as a guest on the Jackie Mason Show. But he's the only Mason I've been involved with. And I renounced his comedy soon after the show."

My Personal Stance

The nit-picking, Pharisaical hyper-critics of Christianity need to be reminded of the wisdom of Gamaliel which he shared with the Sanhedrin Council when they arrested Peter and the apostles and desired to kill them (Acts 5:29-33). Gamaliel stated that if what the followers of Jesus were teaching was false, nothing would come of it. "But if it is of

God, you will not be able to overthrow them." He then added, "You may even be found fighting against God" (Acts 5:38-39).

The pit bulls of Christianity can growl and yap and snarl all they please, but anointed messengers of God like Wilkerson and Cahn will prevail because they are speaking the truth. I stand with them, and I am proud to do so.

Together with them, I cry from the depths of my heart, "Wake up America! You are blaspheming the very God who blessed you. He has sent prophetic voices and remedial judgments to warn you and call you to repentance. What will be your choice? Repentance or Destruction?"

Part 3

A Summary

Chapter 14

Is America Doomed?

> *Then the word of the LORD came to me saying, "Son of man, if a country sins against Me by committing unfaithfulness, and I stretch out My hand against it . . . even though these three men, Noah, Daniel and Job were in its midst, by their own righteousness they could only deliver themselves," declares the Lord GOD.* — Ezekiel 14:12-15

The America I grew up in is gone. It is dead. And there is no hope of its resurrection.

I was born in 1938, and when I was growing up in the 1940s and 50s:

- We went to church three times a week — Sunday morning, Sunday evening and Wednesday evening — and we had four week-long Gospel meetings each year — one each quarter.

- All but the most essential businesses — like hospitals, pharmacies and gasoline stations — were closed on Sundays.

- No secular events, including sporting events, were scheduled on Sunday or on Wednesday evenings.

- We had daily prayers and Bible readings in school, and we celebrated Easter and Christmas with special plays and musicals. We also used readers in our English classes that contained Bible stories. And at graduation time, we had special baccalaureate services where a minister would deliver an inspirational sermon to the graduating class.

- Every public event from court proceedings to city council meetings and PTA meetings were opened with a prayer.

- Movies and television programs were strictly regulated by strong moral codes.

- Our local, state and national leaders talked openly about God and their Christian faith and often led prayers, as President Franklin Roosevelt did on D-Day in 1944 when we invaded the European mainland.

I could go on and on, but I think you get the picture. America was not a perfect nation. Racism was still rampant and materialism was gaining momentum, but we were still a nation that honored and recognized the Christian principles of our forefathers and the founders of our nation. And we were still very aware that our blessings came from God.

The Radically New America

The America of today is radically different, and the changes have taken place with startling rapidity. Incredibly, in just over 50 years since the decade of the 1960s, we have become a nation in full-blown, open rebellion against God. Today:

- We worship the Almighty Dollar.

- Greed has become our national motivator.

- Sex is our obsession.

- Gambling is our national past time.

- We are the world's largest consumer of illegal drugs.

- We have banned God from our schools.

- We have declared God off limits in the public arena.

- We are teaching our children the fantasy of evolution.

- We are slaughtering babies in the name of "freedom of choice' for women.

- We have glamorized homosexuality.

- We have legalized same-sex marriage.

- We are in the process of legalizing marijuana.

- And we have become the moral polluter of planet earth with our violent, immoral and blasphemous movies and TV programs.

In summary, we are a nation that has rejected its Christian heritage and has replaced that precious heritage with a crude, paganized culture. We are a rebellious nation that is thumbing its nose at the Creator God who showered us with unparalleled blessings for over 300 years.

Here's how I summarized it in my book, *Living for Christ in the End Times,* which was originally published in 2000, with a second edition in 2016. The sub-title of the book was "Coping with Anarchy and Apostasy."[1]

> We have expelled God from the life of our society, and the result is an avalanche of wanton violence and immorality. We have lost our moral compass, and we are raising a generation of moral pygmies.

The same is true of the raging apostasy within the Church. The term, Evangelical, has lost its meaning, as some who claim to be Evangelicals are proclaiming that there are many roads to Heaven and there is no Hell.

A Second Reformation is going on in the Church today, but unlike the first, which was based on a call to return to the Bible, this new reformation is calling people to jettison the Bible in behalf of their own feelings and beliefs.

As the Church grows increasingly weak from its internal rot, society continues to plunge into darkness.

I would therefore assert without hesitation that *we are a nation begging for destruction.*

How God Deals With Rebellious Nations

I say that because the Bible clearly reveals that God has a definite way of dealing with rebellious nations which He has richly blessed:

> First, He calls them to repentance through prophetic voices.

> And if the people refuse to respond in repentance, then God will send remedial judgments.

> And if the rebellion persists, there comes *a point of no return* when God will deliver the nation from judgment to destruction.

Consider the example of Nineveh. The prophet Jonah was sent to warn the city of impending destruction, and to his surprise, the king repented and called upon all his people to do likewise. In response, God spared the city. But many years later, God raised up another prophet to send to Nineveh, a prophet named Nahum. This time Nahum was told that Nineveh had **"an incurable wound"** (Nahum 3:19). And sure enough, there was no repentance as before, and the nation was destroyed.

Later, the prophet Jeremiah used the same terminology in reference to Judah (Jeremiah 30:12), and because the nation had reached this tipping point, Jeremiah was told to stop praying for Judah! (Jeremiah 7:16).

Ezekiel was told the same thing, but in stronger terms. He was told that if three of the most righteous men who have ever lived — Noah, Daniel and Job — were to intervene for Judah, it would be of no avail, except for themselves and their families, because the nation had reached the point of no return and was going to be destroyed (Ezekiel 14:12-21).

The Nature of God

Most of the preaching we hear these days about God concerns His grace and love. But there is another side of His nature that is rarely mentioned. He is also a God of righteousness, justice and holiness, and He therefore takes sin very seriously.

He is patient and long-suffering, but He cannot be mocked. He will deal with sin. Consider again these words from Nahum 1:2-3 —

> "A jealous and avenging God is the LORD;
> The LORD is avenging and wrathful.
> The LORD takes vengeance on His adversaries.
> And He reserves wrath for His enemies.
> The LORD is slow to anger and great in power;
> And the LORD will by no means leave the
>   guilty unpunished."

Prophetic Voices to Our Nation

In this book, I have documented in detail how God has patiently sent prophetic voices to call this nation to repentance. But our nation has turned a deaf ear to these prophetic messages. And so, in the 1960s, God began to afflict our nation with remedial judgments designed to get our attention and force us to our knees. They included:

The Vietnam War (1964-1975)

This tragic war, which tore our nation apart, occurred as the sexual revolution of the 1960s was gaining steam.

The 9/11 Attacks (2001)

God allowed the terrorists to be successful in attacking the two symbols of our pride: The Twin Towers in New York which represented our wealth; and the Pentagon in Washington, D.C. which represented our power. But instead of repenting, we responded like a sleepy person by simply hitting the snooze alarm and going back to sleep.

Hurricane Katrina (2005)

Undoubtedly God's response to our immorality and our forcing Israel to abandon the Gaza Strip. The storm formed suddenly in the Gulf on the last day of the Gaza Strip withdrawal and hit New Orleans just as it was getting ready to host its annual homosexual festival.

The September 2008 Stock Market Crash

Again, a response to our attempts to strong arm Israel into surrendering its heartland. It occurred on the eve of Rosh Hashanna, the Jewish New Year, and the market fell by 777 points — indicating the signature of God. (Biblically, 666 is the number of Satan, whereas 777 is a symbol of the Trinity.)

The Type of Leaders We Deserve

It is no accident that President Obama was the most pro-abortion, pro-homosexual, pro-Muslim, anti-Capitalist, anti-Christian, anti-Israel leader in the entire history of our nation.

Clinton vs. Trump

Providing us with the kind of leaders we deserve is a continuing judgment of God upon this nation. Consider, for example, the 2016 presidential election. What a choice!

On the one hand we had a super-liberal, highly deceptive, arrogant, power-hungry, pagan Humanist. On the other hand, we had a crude and rude, gutter-mouth, egotistical Hedonist.

During the campaign, Albert Mohler presented an interesting insight about all this in an editorial on his Internet Blog. He pointed out that 40 years ago in 1976, when Jimmy Carter was running against Gerald Ford, our nation's Evangelical leaders were outraged when Carter became the first presidential candidate to give an interview to *Playboy* magazine.[2]

Now, 40 years later, we had Evangelical leaders who felt they were forced to support the candidacy of a man who was featured on the cover of *Playboy* as the epitome of the playboy lifestyle.

All my friends kept telling me, "Yes, Trump, is awful, but he is the lesser evil." My response was, "How do we know that?" We knew for certain what evil Hillary Clinton believes in. But what did we really know about Trump? He has been on both sides of every issue during his lifetime. How do we know what he really believes about anything?

I thought it was very interesting that during Trump's acceptance speech at the Republican National Convention, he went out of his way to pledge to be a defender of LBGTQ rights — what I call, "The Moral Perversion Movement." He said: "As your president, I will do everything in my power to protect our LGBTQ citizens . . . Believe me." And when a few in the audience applauded, he diverted from his speech and ad-libbed the following comment: "And I have to say, as a Republican, it is so nice to hear you cheering for what I just said. Thank you!"[3]

May I suggest to you that the "lesser evil" might well prove to be the "greater deception"?

To me, the only meaningful difference between the two is that with Hillary, the disintegration of our nation would have accelerated, whereas with Trump, it will slow down, but it will continue.

Trump, in his unmitigated egotism and arrogance says he will "make America great again." That is utter nonsense. The only one who can do that is Jesus, and we have turned our back on Him.

Consider these words spoken by Franklin Graham in Iowa in January 2016 at his very first Decision America rally:[4]

> No political party is going to be able to turn this [our nation] around. I have no hope in the Democratic Party, and listen to me, I have zero hope in the Republican Party. I have no hope in the Tea Party or any other party. My only hope is in Almighty God and His Son, Jesus Christ. The most important thing we can do as Christians is pray.

How can Trump make our nation "great again" when:

- We are murdering 3,000 to 4,000 babies per day?

- We are flooding the world with pornography?

- We are polluting the moral atmosphere of our earth with our violent, immoral and blasphemous movies and TV programs?

- We are promoting and even celebrating sexual

perversion — even to the point of lighting up the White House with the colors of the Sexual Perversion Movement as a way of celebrating the abominable same-sex marriage decision of our Supreme Court?

God's Pattern of Destruction

There are many Christians in our nation who refuse to believe that God will ever touch us — that He will ever allow us to be destroyed. They tend to think that God sits on His throne draped in an American flag. But, my friends, God cannot be deceived. He will not tolerate unrepented sin.

The Jews of ancient Judah thought the same thing about their nation. When Jeremiah warned them of imminent destruction, they cried out, "The Temple, the Temple" (Jeremiah 7:4), meaning they did not believe that God would ever allow anyone to destroy His Temple. But He did.

God is gracious. He is longsuffering. He warns and warns before He pours out judgment and ultimate destruction, but he will not tolerate unrepented sin.

He loves our nation. He was the One who raised it up on the foundation of His Word. He is the One who has blessed it so abundantly. He is the One who worked through us to spread the Gospel all over the world. But the Word of God says: "To those to whom much is given, much is expected" (Luke 12:48).

Our nation is in full-blown rebellion against God, and God is not going to tolerate it much longer. We are now in open rebellion against God — cursing Him and shaking our fist at Him and mocking His Son.

Romans chapter one reveals how God deals with a nation He has blessed that rises up in rebellion against Him.

Romans 1:18-20

18) For the wrath of God is revealed from heaven against all ungodliness and unrighteousness of men who suppress the truth in unrighteousness,

19) because that which is known about God is evident within them; for God made it evident to them.

20) For since the creation of the world His invisible attributes, His eternal power and divine nature, have been clearly seen, being understood through what has been made, so that they are without excuse.

Now, what do these verses say? They are saying that the wrath of God is reserved for any nation that rejects God in attitude and actions and suppresses the truth about Him. And they further say that there is no excuse for denying the existence of God because God has given to each person an innate knowledge of His existence and has made that existence apparent to them in His Creation.

Is America a nation guilty of "suppressing the truth in unrighteousness"? Absolutely! We refuse to allow our children to be taught the true origin of the universe and the true origin of life. Instead, we indoctrinate them with the lies of Evolution and teach them that life in the womb is of no value.

We have started filtering out of our history books the truth regarding the Christian foundation of our nation. And we are teaching them to worship the Creation rather than the Creator.

Beginning with verse 24 in Romans 1, we are told how God deals with such a rebellious nation. He steps back and lowers the hedge of protection around the nation and allows sin to multiply in the form of a sexual revolution:

Romans 1:24

"Therefore God gave them [those in rebellion] over in the lusts of their hearts to impurity, so that their bodies would be dishonored among them."

This is exactly what happened to our nation in the 1960s when we experienced the Sexual Revolution.

If this action proves insufficient to produce repentance, then Romans 1 says that God will take a second step back and lower the hedge of protection even farther:

Romans 1:26-27

26) For this reason God gave them over to degrading passions; for their women exchanged the natural function for that which is unnatural,

27) and in the same way also the men abandoned the natural function of the woman and burned in their desire toward one another, men with men committing indecent acts and receiving in their own persons the due penalty of their error.

So, the result of the second step back is a plague of homosexuality. We have been in this second phase ever since the Supreme Court struck down all the state laws against sodomy in 2003.

Romans 1 continues by revealing what God will do if the rebellious nation sets its jaw and continues to rebel against God and His Word. God will step back a third time and lower the hedge of protection again, and according to Romans 1:28, He will deliver the nation over to a "depraved mind," at which point the nation will either destroy itself or be destroyed by an outside force.

I believe we have reached that point here in this nation.

How else can you explain the transgender bathroom issue? Transgenders are mentally ill. A man calling himself a woman is as deceived and mentally deranged as one who says he is Elvis or Jesus. Yet our society is caving in to the demands of the Moral Perversion Movement by allowing transgenders to use the bathroom of their choice.

God in His grace may have decided to give us a little more breathing time, in order that more might be saved, but there is a limit to His patience.

This is exactly what He did with ancient Judah. Following the worst king in their history, King Manasseh, who ruled for 55 years. God raised up a righteous king named Josiah who reigned 31 years and led a national spiritual revival. But when Josiah was killed on the battlefield, the nation immediately fell back into its rebellious ways, and God destroyed it.

The problem was that evil had become too ingrained in the fabric of the nation.

And I believe that is where we are today. If you don't think so, then consider these chilling facts. *Despite the most ungodly presidency in American history:*

1) President Obama left office with a 60% approval rating.

2) His designate heir, Hillary Clinton, received 3 million more votes than Trump.

3) The Millennials of our nation — those between the ages of 18 and 29 — supported a Socialist, and when he failed to win the nomination, they voted overwhelmingly for Clinton (55%). These young people are the future of our nation!

And if that is not enough, just go to Google and type in the word, Christianity, and start reading the articles. You will find one hate-filled article after another attacking Christianity, Christians, Jesus, and Christian leaders like Franklin Graham.

I would contend that these brutal realities indicate where the heart of America really is today.

Is There Any Hope for America?

All of which brings me back to the crucial question: Is there any hope left for our nation?

My answer is, "How could there be?"

We have turned our back on God and rejected the very One who gave us all our blessings.

And we need to be clear as to why that happened. It was not due to the attacks of the Secularists, the Humanists, the Atheists or the Sexual Libertarians. No, it has been due to the failure of the Church to preach the Gospel, call people to repentance and stand for righteousness. In short, the Church has sought popular approval, and in the process, it has gotten in bed with the world.

The Bible prophesies in many places that the end times will be characterized by major apostasy — and we are up to our ears in it right now. It all began in the 1920s when our seminaries were captivated by the German School of Higher Criticism which argued that the Bible is not God's revealed word, but instead, it is Man's search for God and is thus filled with myths, legends, superstitions and errors.

This produced the liberal Social Gospel that soon came to characterize the mainline denominations as they focused on social and political action rather than the preaching of the Gospel. This spiritual virus has since spread to the Evangelical sector of American Christianity in the form of the Emergent Church Movement.

In the mid-20th Century, to be an Evangelical meant that the Bible was your source of authority for all beliefs and actions. Today, the term, Evangelical, has lost its meaning because there are professing Evangelicals who believe:

- The Scriptures contain errors and contradictions.

- There is no Hell.

- There are many roads to God.

- Homosexuality is a valid lifestyle.

- Evolution is the true explanation of life.

- The ultimate purpose of the Church is not the salvation of souls but the saving of our planet.

It is no wonder that our nation is wallowing in spiritual darkness and rebellion against God. And how can anyone truly believe there is any hope for our nation in the midst of such gross spiritual apostasy?

Here's how I put it in my *Prophetic Manifesto*:[5]

> We have turned our back on the very God who made us great and showered us with blessings. We have forgotten that God's Word teaches that "to those to whom much is given, much is expected" (Luke 12:47-48).

> We have stubbornly set our course. We have determined to live as we please and not as God has dictated. We have chartered a course of self-destruction, and God is going to allow us to have our way.

A Chilling Thought

Let me share a chilling thought with you. Our nation is more divided than it has been since 1861. We have the two coasts against the heartland.

Also, people have been in the streets demonstrating ever since Trump was elected, and they are still there. Our nation has been swept with a spirit of anger and rebellion. And to make it all even worse, President Trump keeps pouring gasoline on the fire with his caustic comments and personal attacks on his critics.

This could easily lead to blood in the streets, martial law, and even to civil war. And in that regard, Trump could prove to be God's hammer of wrath on this nation.

Hope for Believers and Unbelievers

But there is good news in the midst of the growing spiritual darkness and the consequent decay of our society.

There is *individual* hope for those of us who know Jesus as our Lord and Savior. God has promised repeatedly in His Word that He will never forsake us. For example, in Isaiah 43 He has promised to walk with us through the fire and high water, comforting us in our sufferings and providing our needs (Isaiah 43:2-3). And consider this promise: "The LORD is the one who goes ahead of you; He will be with you. He will not fail you or forsake you. Do not fear or be dismayed" (Deuteronomy 31:8).

We also have the incredible hope of the Rapture of the Church when true believers will be taken out of this world in the blinking of an eye to be with Jesus forever.

There is also individual hope for those who do not know Jesus. As Robert Jeffress has pointed out, when the darkness deepens, the light of Jesus will shine more brightly, like a diamond on a black cloth, and more and more people will be drawn to Jesus as their hearts are penetrated by the Gospel.

The message of the Holy Spirit for **believers** in these end times is twofold: Commit your lives to holiness and share the

Gospel with as many people as you can, as quickly as you can.

The message of the Spirit for **unbelievers** is, "Jesus is coming soon. He is returning to pour out the wrath of God on those who have rejected the grace, mercy and love of God. Reach out now and receive Him in faith as your Lord and Savior before it is too late."

Ironic Good News

I must add that there is an ironic way in which there is good news that can be derived from the collapse of civilization all around us.

It can be found in the statement of Jesus in Matthew 24:37-38 where He said His return would occur at a time when society has gone full circle back to the immorality and violence that characterized the days of Noah. In 1996 a federal judge named Robert Bork published a book about the moral drift of our nation that was titled, *Slouching Towards Gomorrah.*

Well, we are no longer slouching. *We have arrived.* And that terrible fact points to the good news that Jesus is returning soon.

Conclusion

In conclusion, let me say we live in the midst of an increasingly secular and evil society — a society that calls good evil and evil good. As we look around the world today, we can see that evil is multiplying. It is as if the whole world is falling to pieces.

But the truth is that from a biblical perspective, as Jan Markell has put it, *the pieces are all falling into place for Jesus to return.*

Which is why the great pastor, Adrian Rogers, once said, "The world is growing gloriously dark."[6]

As we wait for Jesus' return, we need to realize that all of us have been desensitized to some degree by the sin that is abounding around us and to our participation in it. And thus, before we go forth to confront the evil in society, we need to face up to it in our own lives and respond in repentance. Righteousness must begin in our hearts before we challenge the unrighteousness of society.

And as we confront society, we should expect increasing hostility and persecution. But the Bible assures us that God will sustain us. Consider these words from Psalm 34:

> 15) The eyes of the LORD are toward the righteous
> And His ears are open to their cry.
>
> 16) The face of the LORD is against evildoers,
> To cut off the memory of them from the earth.
>
> 17) The righteous cry, and the LORD hears
> And delivers them out of all their troubles.
>
> 18) The LORD is near to the brokenhearted
> And saves those who are crushed in spirit.
>
> 19) Many are the afflictions of the righteous,
> But the LORD delivers him out of them all.
>
> 22) The LORD redeems the soul of His servants, And none of those who take refuge in Him will be condemned.

Let us, therefore, keep our eyes focused on Jesus, for He is "the author and perfecter of our faith, who for the joy set before Him endured the cross, despising the shame, and has sat down at the right hand of the throne of God" (Hebrews 12:2).

In summary, as we await the Lord's return, we are:

- To stand for righteousness.
- To pray for courage.

- To commit to holiness.

- To share the Gospel.

- And we are to put our trust in Jesus and in Him alone.

And don't forget to cry out daily, "Maranatha, Maranatha, Maranatha! Come quickly, Lord Jesus!" (1 Corinthians 16: 22).

About the Author

Dr. David R. Reagan is the Senior Evangelist for Lamb & Lion Ministries, a Bible prophecy ministry located in the Dallas, Texas area.

Before founding the ministry in 1980, Dr. Reagan served for 20 years as a university professor, teaching international law and politics. Throughout that time he was an ardent student of the Bible. All his advanced degrees were earned at The Fletcher School of Law & Diplomacy, a graduate school of international relations in the Boston area that is owned and operated jointly by Tufts and Harvard Universities.

Since 1980 Dr. Reagan has taught Bible prophecy in meetings and seminars held all across America and around the world. His weekly television program, "Christ in Prophecy," is broadcast both nationally and internationally.

He has led over 45 pilgrimages to Israel and is considered to be an expert on Middle East politics and Israel in Bible prophecy.

Dr. Reagan has been gifted with the skill to communicate complex ideas in simple, understandable terms. He is the author of 15 books, including one of the only children's books ever published about end time Bible prophecy. It is titled *Jesus Is Coming Again!*

Dr. Reagan and his wife, Ann, have been married more than 55 years. They live in a suburb of Dallas, Texas. They are the parents of two daughters and have four grandchildren and two great grandsons.

You can find more detailed information about every aspect of Lamb & Lion Ministries at the ministry's website: www.lamblion.com.

Photo Credits

Page 27 — Peter Marshall, Getty images, photo by Francis Miller, The LIFE Picture Collection.

Page 45 — David Wilkerson, www.pinterest.com/pin/50975125 1546905495.

Page 59 — Francis Schaeffer, painting by John Robinette and is used with his permission and the permission of Tyndale Publishers.

Page 77 — Aleksandr Solzhenitsyn, Alamy Images, www.alamy. com/stock-photo-dpa-files-soviet-author-aleksandr-solzhenitsyn-pictured-in-bonn-germany-53728108. html.

Page 93 — Donald Wildmon, photo courtesy of The American Family Association, www.afa.net.

Page 109 — Erwin Lutzer, photo courtesy of The Moody Church in Chicago, Illinois, www.moodychurch.org.

Page 125 — David Jeremiah, photo courtesy of Shadow Mountain Church in El Cajon, California, www.shadowmount ain.org.

Page 141 — William Koenig, photo supplied by Bill Koenig, https:// watch.org.

Page 157 — Jan Markell, photo supplied by Jan Markell, www.olive treeviews.org.

Page 173 — Albert Mohler, Jr., www.albertmohler.com.

Page 187 — Franklin Graham, photo courtesy of The Billy Graham Evangelistic Association, https://billygraham.org.

Page 203 — Robert Jeffress, photo courtesy of First Baptist Church in Dallas, Texas, www.firstdallas.org.

Page 223 — Jonathan Cahn, photo supplied by Jonathan Cahn, www.hopeoftheworld.org.

References

Prologue: America's Spiritual Crisis

1) American Humanist Association, "Humanist Manifesto I," https://americanhumanist.org/what-is-humanism/manifesto1.

2) Ibid., page 2.

3) Ibid.

4) Ibid.

5) Ibid, page 3.

6) Ibid.

7) Ibid., page 4.

8) American Humanist Association, "Humanist Manifesto II," https://americanhumanist.org/what-is-humanism/manifesto2, page 1.

9) Ibid.

10) Ibid.

11) Ibid., page 2.

12) Ibid.

13) Ibid.

14) Ibid., page 3.

15) Ibid.

16) Ibid., page 4.

17) Ibid.

18) Ibid., page 5.

19) Ibid., page 6.

20) American Humanist Association, "Humanism and Its Aspirations: Humanist Manifesto III, a Successor to the Humanist Manifesto of 1933," https://americanhumanist.org/what-is-humanism/manifesto3.

21) Ibid.

22) Wikipedia, "Paul Kurtz," https://en.wikipedia.org/wiki/Paul_Kurtz.

23) Council for Secular Humanism, "A Secular Humanist Declaration Issued In 1980 by The Council for Democratic and Secular Humanism (now the Council for Secular Humanism)," www.secularhumanism.org/index.php/ 11, page 4.

24) Ibid., page 1.

25) International Humanist and Ethical Union, "The Amsterdam Declaration 1952," http://iheu.org/humanism/the-amsterdam-declaration/the-amsterdam -declaration-1952.

26) Ibid., page 3.

27) Ibid., page 2.

28) Ibid., page 3.

29) International Humanist and Ethical Union, "The Amsterdam Declaration 2002," http://iheu.org/humanism/the-amsterdam-declaration.

30) Ibid., page 1.

31) Ibid.

32) Ibid., page 2.

33) Ibid.

34) Eagle Forum, "Secular Humanists Give Dunphy Another Platform," http:// eagleforum.org/educate/1995/nov95/dunphy.html, page 1.

35) Ibid.

36) Ibid.

37) John J. Dunphy, "The Book That Started It All," *Secular Humanist Bulletin*, Volume 21, Number 4 (Winter 2005/2006), www.secularhumanism.org/ index.php/articles/3452, page 2.

38) All About . . . "Secular Humanism — Excluding God from Schools & Society," www.allaboutphilosophy.org/secular-humanism.htm, page 1.

39) U.S. Supreme Court, "Church of the Holy Trinity v. United States, 143, U.S. 457 (1892)," https://supreme.justia.com/cases/federal/us/143/457case. html, page 14.

40) Dr. Robert Schultz, "A Christian America: Earl Warren and Our Christian Roots," https://chalcedon.edu/magazine/a-christian-america-earl-warren- and-our-christian-roots, pages 1-2.

41) *The Jackson Press*, "'America needs God more than God needs America,' Reagan stated, 'If we ever forget that we are One Nation Under God, then we will be a Nation gone under,'" February 7, 2017, http://thejackson press.org/?p=61748.

42) Jim Garlow, Transcription of a speech to the National Religious Broadcast- ers Convention in Februay-March of 2010 in Nashville, Tennessee.

43) William F.Buckley, Jr., *God and Man at Yale*, (Washington, D.C.: Regnery Publishing, 1951)

Chapter 1: Peter Marshall

1) Catherine Marshall, *A Man Called Peter* (New York, NY: McGraw-Hill Book Company, 1951).

2) Peter Marshall, "Trial by Fire." Permission to reprint this edited version of Marshall's sermon was granted by his son, Peter John Marshall, before his death in 2010. This version of the sermon is based on a transcription of an audio program.

3) Editorial in *Life* magazine, December 27, 1943 (Vol. 15, No. 26) page 28.

4) John Dart, "Billy Graham Recalls Help From Hearst," *Los Angeles Times*, June 7, 1997, http://articles.latimes.com/1997-06-07/local/me-1034_1_ billy-graham-recalls.

Chapter 2: David Wilkerson

1) David Wilkerson, with John and Elizabeth Sherrill, *The Cross and the Switchblade* (New York, NY: Jove Books, 1962).

2) Gateway Films, *The Cross and the Switchblade*, 1970.

3) David Wilkerson, *The Vision* (Old Tappan, NJ: Pyramid Publications for Fleming H. Revell Company, 1974).

4) Ibid., page 1.

5) Ibid., page 15.

6) Ibid., page 17.

7) Ibid., page 18.

8) Ibid.

9) Ibid., page 21.

10) Ibid., page 22,

11) Ibid., pages 31-32,

12) Ibid., page 43.

13) Ibid., page 45.

14) Ibid..

15) Ibid., page 47.

16) Ibid., page 48.

17) Ibid., page

18) Ibid., page 78.

19) Ibid., page 52.

20) Ibid., pages 63, 66 & 70.

21) Ibid., page 64.

22) Ibid., page 68.

23) Ibid., page 75.

24) Ibid.

25) Ibid., page 86.

26) Ibid., page 32.

27) Ibid., page 87.

28) Ibid., pages 44 & 45.

29) Ibid., page 41.

Chapter 3: Francis Schaeffer

1) Susan Le Gras Davis, "Dr. Francis Schaeffer: God's Man for this Era," Good News Publishers, *PIONEER* magazine, July-August 1984, page 1.

2) Cal Thomas, "Francis August Schaeffer, IV: Crusader for Truth," *The*

Fundamentalist Journal, July-August, 1984, page 48.

3) Ibid.

4) The Orthodox Presbyterian Church of America, "Today in OPC History, January 30, 2012 Francis Schaeffer," www.opc.org/today.html?history-id=740, page 2.

5) Louis Gifford Parkhurst, Jr, *Francis Schaeffer: The Man and His Message* (Wheaton, IL: Tyndale House Publishers, 1985), page 28.

6) Edith Schaeffer, *The Tapestry* (Waco, TX: Word Books, 1981), page 52.

7) Parkhurst, pages 37-38.

8) Ibid., page 47.

9) OPC, "Today in OPC History . . ." page 1.

10) Ibid.

11) Hamilton, page 2.

12) Parkhurst, page 58.

13) Ibid., pages 63-64.

14) Harold Fickett, "Our Contentious Catalyst: Francis Schaeffer never stopped battling for the faith," *Christianity Today* magazine, November 20, 2008, www.christianitytoday.com/ct/2008/november/29.73.html, page 2.

15) Parkhurst, page 70.

16) Francis Schaeffer, *How Should We Then Live?* (Old Tappan, NJ: Revell, 1976). Film by the same title issued by Gospel Films and produced by Billy Zeoli and Frank Schaeffer, V.

17) Francis Schaeffer, *How Should We Then Live?: The Rise and Decline of Western Thought and Culture,* L'Abri 50th Anniversary Edition (Wheaton, IL: Crossway Books, 2005), page 71.

18) Ibid., page 121.

19) Schaeffer, film version of *HSWTL?* Part 8: "The Age of Fragmentation."

20) Francis Schaeffer, "A Review of a Review," in *The Bible Today* magazine, October 1948, pages 7-9.

21) Schaeffer, *HSWTL?* page 205.

22) Schaeffer, film version of *HSWTL?* Part 9: "The Age of Personal Peace and Affluence."

23) Schaeffer, *HSWTL?* page 245.

24) Schaeffer, film version of *HSWTL?* Part 10: "Final Choices."

25) Schaeffer, *HSWTL?* page 258.

26) C. Everett Koop and Francis Schaeffer, *Whatever Happened to the Human*

Race? (Westchester, IL: Crossway Books, 1979).

27) Ibid., page v.

28) Ibid., page 1.

29) Ibid.

30) Ibid., page 7.

31) Ibid., page 81.

32) Ibid., chapters 6 & 7, pages 129-149.

33) Francis Schaeffer, *A Christian Manifesto* (Wheaton, IL: Crossway Books, 1981).

34) Ibid., page 10.

35) Ibid., page 23.

36) Ibid., page 27.

37) Ibid., pages 31-39.

38) Ibid., page 41.

39) Ibid.

40) Ibid., page 49.

41) Ibid., pages 89-102.

42) Ibid., page 120.

43) Ibid., page 124.

44) Ibid., page 112.

45) Ibid., page 116.

46) Ibid., page 73.

47) Ibid., page 79.

48) Ibid., page 74.

49) Ibid., pages 81 and 110.

50) Ibid., page 110.

51) Francis Schaeffer, *The Great Evangelical Disaster* (Wheaton, IL: Crossway Books, 1984).

52) Francis Schaeffer, "Who Are The True Revolutionaries?" *Biblical Missions* magazine, February 1948, www.thisday.pcahistory.org/author/archivist, page 2.

53) Schaeffer, *Evangelical Disaster*, page 37.

54) Ibid.

55) Ibid.

56) Ibid., page 44.

57) Ibid., page 46.

58) Matthew Barrett, "The Great Evangelical Disaster," *Credo* magazine, October 9, 2012, www.credomag.com/2012/10/19/the-great-evangelical-disaster, page 2.

59) Schaeffer, *Evangelical Disaster*, pages 31-32.

60) Parkhurst, page 27.

Chapter 4: Aleksandr Solzhenitsyn

1) Aleksandr Solzhenitsyn, *One Day in the Life of Ivan Denisovich*, (New York, NY: Penguin Books, 1963).

2) Aleksandr Solzhenitsyn, *Cancer Ward,* (New York,NY: Dial Press, 1968).

3) Max Hayward and Edward L. Crowley, eds., *Soviet Literature in the Sixties* (London: Methuen Books, 1965), page 191.

4) Wikipedia, "Aleksandr Solzhenitsyn," https://en.wikipedia.org/wiki/Aleksandr_ Solzhenitsyn, page 11.

5) Nobel Prize Foundation, www.nobelprize.org/search/?query=1970.

6) Aleksandr Solzhenitsyn, *The Gulag Archipelago* (Paris, France: Éditions du Seuil, 1973 in Russian). First English publication in 1974 by Harper & Row in New York, NY.

7) *The Economist* magazine, "Aleksander Solzhenitsyn: Speaking truth to power," April 7, 2008, www.economist.com/node/11885318, page 1.

8) David Aikman, "Profiles in Faith: Aleksandr Solzhenitsyn, Part II: A World Split Apart: Solzhenitsyn's Harvard Speech Twenty-four Years Later," www.cslewisinstitute.org, page 1.

9) Ibid.

10) Brian C. Anderson, "Solzhenitsyn's Permanence," www.newcriterion. com/articles.cfm/Solzhenitsyn-s-permanence-8077, page 1.

11) Ibid.

12) American Rhetoric Online Speech Bank, "Aleksandr Solzhenitsyn: 'A World Split Apart,' Address at Harvard University on June 8, 1978," http://americanrhetoric.com/speeches/alexandersolzhenitsynharvard.htm, page 4.

13) Ibid., page 5.

14) Ibid., page 6.

15) Ibid., pages 6-7.

16) Ibid., page 8.

17) Ibid., page 10.

18) Ibid.

19) Ibid., page 11.

20) Ibid., page 12.

21) Unsigned editorial, "Solzhenitsyn Flays the West," *Harvard Magazine,* April 25, 2011.

22) David Aikman, page 1.

23) NobelPrize.org, "Lists of Nobel Prizes and Laureates: 1970," www.nobel prize.org/search/?query=1970.

24) Aleksandr Solzhenitsyn, "'Men Have Forgotten God' — The Templeton Address," May 1983, www.roca.org/OA/36/36h.htm.

25) Ibid., page 1.

26) Ibid.

27) Ibid.

28) Ibid., page 3.

29) Ibid.

30) Ibid.

31) Ibid., pages 3-4.

32) Ibid., page 4.

Chapter 5: Donald Wildmon

1) Donald Wildmon and Randall Nulton, *Don Wildmon: The Man the Networks Love to Hate* (Wilmore, KY: Bristol Books, 1989) page 157.

2) Ibid., page 165.

3) Ibid., pages 165-166.

4) Ibid., page 168.

5) Ibid., pages 148-149.

6) Don Wildmon with Allen Wildmon, *I Had A Vision; God Had A Plan* (Tupelo, Mississippi: American Family Association, 2013), page 149.

7) Wildmon & Nulton, page 170.

8) Ibid., page 171.

9) Ibid., pages 43-55.

10) Ted Ownby, "Donald Wildmon, the American Family Association, and the Theology of Media Activism," http://livedtheology.org/wp-content/uploads/2012/10/ownby_wildmon_paper4.pdf, undated, page 25.

11) Billy Dave and Steve Jordahl, "The preacher who caused heartburn in Hollywood," www.onenewsnow.com, March 3, 2017, page 1.

12) Wildmon & Wildmon, page 12.

13) Ibid., page 14.

14) Wildmon & Nulton, pages 26-28.

15) Wildmon & Wildmon, page 59.

16) Ibid., page 14.

17) Wildmon & Nulton, pages 43-55.

18) Wildmon & Wildmon, pages 213-214.

19) Ibid., page 214.

20) Ibid.

21) Ibid., page 215.

22) Ibid.

23) Ibid.

24) Ibid., page 215.

25) Ibid.

26) Ibid., pages 221-223.

27) Ibid., pages 223-224.

28) Ibid., page 225.

29) Day & Jordahl, page 1.

30) Ibid.

31) Wildmon & Wildmon, page xii.

32) Ibid.

33) Ibid.

34) Ibid., page 149.

35) Wikipedia, "American Family Association," https://en.wikipedia.org/wiki/ American_Family_Association, page 1.

36) Dave & Jordahl, page 2.

37) Wikipedia, "Donald Wildmon," https://en.wikipedia.org/wiki/Donald_Wild mon, page 1.

38) Family Research Council, "Prayer Targets: "Will the Church Forget?" www.frc.org/prayerteam/prayer-targets-will-the-church-forget-watchmen -on-the-wall-call2fall-boy-scouts, May 29, 2013, page 1.

39) Personal conversation with Don Wildmon in the 1980s.

40) Dave & Jordahl, page 2.

41) Ownby, page 25.

42) Anna Wolfe, "Inside the AFA: How One 'Hate Group' Is Fighting The 'Gay Agenda,'" pages 2-3.

43) Wildmon & Wildmon, pages 110-111.

Chapter 6: Erwin Lutzer

1) Erwin W. Lutzer, *When A Nation Forgets God: 7 Lessons We Must Learn from Nazi Germany* (Chicago, IL: Moody Publishers, 2010).

2) Moody Church, "Dr. Erwin W. Lutzer," www.moodychurch.org/staff-directory/erwin-w-lutzer.

3) Ibid.

4) Ed Stetzer, "Sunday Journeys — Serving as Interim at Moody Church," July 17, 2016, www.christianitytoday.com/edstetzer/2016/july/sunday-journeys-serving-as-interim-pastor-at-moody-church.html.

5) John Ankerberg, "Dr. Erwin Lutzer – A Personal Testimony." www.jashow.org/articles/guests-and-authors/dr-john-ankerberg/dr-erwin-lutzer-%E2%80%93-a-personal-testimony/, page 1.

6) Lutzer, *"When A Nation Forgets God . . ."* pages 35-55.

7) Erwin Lutzer, "America's Spiritual Crisis," http://articles.ochristian.com/article3157.shtml, page 1.

8) Ibid.

9) Ibid.

10) Ibid.

11) Ibid.

12) Ibid., pages 1-2.

13) Lutzer, *"When A Nation Forgets God . . ."* page 9.

14) Ibid., pages 9-10.

15) Viktor Frankl, *The Doctor and the Soul: Introduction to Logotherapy* (New York: Knopf, 1982), page xxi.

16) Lutzer, *"When A Nation Forgets God . . ."* page 11.

17) Ibid., pages 16-33.

18) Ibid., page 24.

19) Ibid., pages 36-55.

20) Ibid., page 47

21) Ibid., pages 57-74.

22) Ibid., pages 61-62.

23) Ibid., pages 75-95.

24) Ibid., page 81.

25) Ibid., pages 97-115.

26) Ibid., page 99.

27) Ibid., pages 117-130.

28) Ibid., pages 117-119.

29) Ibid., pages 131-141.

30) Ibid., pages 135-136.

31) Ibid., page 137.

32) Alchetron, "The Great Dictator," https://alchetron.com/The-Great-Dictator-19657-W, page 15.

Chapter 7: David Jeremiah

1) David Jeremiah, *I Never Thought I'd See The Day!* (New York, Boston, Nashville: Faith Works, 2011) page xiv.

2) Ibid.

3) Ibid.

4) David Jeremiah, *Is This The End?* (Nashville, TN: W. Publishing Group, 2016), pages 103-105.

5) "Biography of Dr. David Jeremiah," www.davidjeremiah.org/site/about/biography.aspx.

6) Jeremiah, *Day!* page xiii.

7) Ibid., page xix.

8) Ibid.

9) Ibid., pages xv-xvii.

10) Ibid, page 4.

11) Ibid., page 38.

12) Ibid., page 90.

13) Ibid., page 101.

14) Ibid., page 127.

15) Ibid., page 158.

16) Ibid., page 201.

17) Ibid., page 242.

18) Ibid., pages 274-275.

19) Jeremiah, *End?* page vii.

20) Ibid.

21) Ibid.

22) Ibid., page 15.

23) Ibid.

24) Ibid., page 18.

25) Ibid., page 20.

26) Ibid., page 29.

27) Ibid., pages 57-86.

28) Ibid., page 61-66.

29) Ibid., page 62.

30) Ibid., page 63.

31) Ibid., pages 63-64.

32) Ibid., pages 64-65.

33) Ibid., pages 65-66.

34) Ibid., page x.

35) Ibid.

36) Ibid., pages 117-143.

37) Erwin W. Lutzer, *Will America Be Given Another Chance?* (Chicago, IL: Moody Press, 1993).

38) Jeremiah, *End?* pages 125-141.

39) Ibid., pages 120-124.

40) Ibid., page 140.

41) Ibid., pages 237-268.

42) Ibid., page 285.

Chapter 8: William Koenig

1) Personal email message from Bill Koenig to the author dated April 20, 2017.

2) Ibid.

3) Ibid.

4) "About William Koenig," http://williamkoenig.com/about, page 1.

5) Ibid., page 2.

6) Ibid.

7) William Koenig, *Eye to Eye: Facing the Consequences of Dividing Israel* (McLean, VA: About Him Publishing, 2004).

8) Amos 3:7, "Replacement Denominations." http://amos37.com/replacement-denominations, page 2.

9) Ibid., page 3.

10) Leslie F. Church, editor, *Commentary on the Whole Bible by Matthew Henry* (Grand Rapids, MI: Zondervan Publishing House, 1961), page 906.

11) William Koenig, *Eye to Eye: Facing the Consequences of Dividing Israel* (McLean, VA: About Him Publishing, revised and updated edition, 2008), pages 40-41.

12) Ibid., pages 41-42.

13) Ibid., pages 80-81, 84-85.

14) Ibid., pages 100-101.

15) Ibid., pages 111-112, 168.

16) Ibid., pages 115-124, 168.

17) Ibid., back cover.

18) Ibid., pages 149-154.

19) Ibid., page 150.

20) William Koenig, *Revealed: Obama's Legacy* (McLean, VA: Christian Publications, 2016).

21) Ibid., page 146.

22) Ibid., page 176.

23) Ibid., page 14.

24) Ibid., page 49.

25) Ibid., page 21.

26) Ibid., pages 94-106.

27) Ibid., page 16.

28) Ibid., page 68.

29) Ibid., pages 132-133.

30) Ibid., page 106, quoting Stoyan Zaimov, "Bill Maher Says Obama Is Really an Atheist, Mocks Hillary Clinton's Devotion to The Bible" www.christianpost.com/news/bill-maher-says-obama-is-really-an-atheist-mocks-hillary-clintons-devotion-to-the-bible-122118/#sJplrDrwQVZarq0I.99.

31) William Koenig, *Revealed*, page 145.

32) Bill Koenig, "Heredity of Sin," May 30, 2010, www.williamkoenig.com/content/2010/05/30/heredity-of-sin, page 1.

33) Ibid.

34) Bill Koenig, "How Harvard, Yale, and Columbia are leading us to Armageddon." May 10, 2010 www.williamkoenig.com/content/2010/03/ 20/543, page 1.

35) Ibid.

Chapter 9: Jan Markell

1) Personal email message from Jan Markell to the author dated April 24, 2017, page 2.

2) Ibid.

3) Ibid.

4) Ibid.

5) Jan Markell, "An Open Door Closes," April 4, 2017, www.olivetreeviews. org/news/headlines/item/12501-an-open-door-closes-jan-markell, page 1.

6) Email message, April 24, 2017, page 3.

7) Ibid.

8) Ibid.

9) Ibid.

10) Worldview Times, "Jan Markell," http://old.worldviewweekend.com/world view-times/bio.php?authorid=23.

11) Email message, April 24, 2017, page 3.

12) Jan Markell, "Replacement Theology Leads to Replacement Reality," January 8, 2008, www.moriel.org/articles-new/2015-12-06-13-34-02/jan-markell/item/706-replacement-theology-leads-to-replacement-reality.html,, page 1.

13) Ibid.

14) Ibid., page 2.

15) Ibid.

17) Jan Markell, "The Dual Covenant Heresy: More End-Time Deception," October 28, 2008, www.bibleprophecyblog.com/2008/10/dual-covenant-heresy-more-end-time.html, page 1.

18) Ibid., page 2.

19) Ibid.

20) *Understanding the Times*, "Why America is Absent from Bible Prophecy," by Jan Markell, September-October 2015, page 3.

21) Ibid.

22) *Understanding the Times*, "2016: The Year America Betrayed Her Best Friend," by Jan Markell, January-February 2017, page 1.

23) Ibid.

24) Ibid., page 2.

25) Email message, April 24, 2017, page 4.

26) Ibid.

27) Jan Markell, "Liberal Evangelicals Don't Represent me!" November 24, 2011, www.wnd.com/2011/11/371169, page 1.

28) Ibid.

29) Jan Markell, "The NAE Heads Left," March 21, 2007, www.omegaletter.

com/articles/articles.asp?ArticleID=6084, page 2.

30) Ibid.

31) Markell, "Liberal Evangelicals . . ." page 1.

32) Ibid., page 2.

33) Jan Markell, "When Evangelicals Dine with the Wicked," August 18, 2009, www.moriah.com.au/textarchive/willow-creek-leadership-summit-2009. htm.

34) Ibid., page 2.

35) Jan Markell, "The Emergent Church: A Dangerous Fad or Solid New Movement?" January 11, 2008, www.omegaletter.com/articles/articles.asp? ArticleID=5390, page 1.

36) Ibid.

37) Jan Markell, "The New Evangelicalism," November 5, 2007, http://old. worldviewweekend.com/worldview-times/print.php?&ArticleID=2680, page 1.

38) Ibid.

39) Bethel University, "About the University," www.bethel.edu/about.

40) Jan Markell, "Bethel University Throws Students to Interspiritual Wolves," November 10, 2009, www.lighthouse trailsresearch.com/blog/?p=191, page 1.

41) Jan Markell, "When Contending Costs Everything," January 18, 2011, www.bibleprophecyblog.com/2011/01/when-contending-costs-everything. html, pages 2-3.

42) Jan Markell, "An Open Letter to Pastor Rick Warren," September 4, 2009, www.olivetreeviews.org/e-updates/jans-articles?start=30, page 1.

43) Ibid., page 2.

44) Ibid, page 1.

45) Ibid., page 2.

46) Ibid.

47) Ibid.

48) Jan Markell, "When Contending Costs Everything," page 1.

49) Ibid.

50) Mike Oppenheimer, "To Defend the Truth," www.letusreason.org/defend-truth.htm, page 3.

51) Ibid., page 4.

52) Jan Markell, "America Distances God," January 3, 2008, www.omegaletter. com/articles/articles.asp?ArticleID= 6221, page 1.

53) Ibid., pages 1-2.

54) *Understanding the Times*, "Who Are the Masters of Deceit?" by Jan Markell, November-December 2015, pages 4-5.

55) *Understanding the Times*, "Things Aren't Falling Apart — They're Falling in Place," by Jan Markell, January-February 2015, page 1.

56) *Understanding the Times*, "The Sea and the Waves Roaring," by Jan Markell, November-December 2016, page 2.

Chapter 10: Albert Mohler, Jr.

1) Denny Burk, "Documentary on Albert Mohler's Presidency," video produced in 2013, www.dennyburk.com/must-see-documentary-on-albert-moh lers-presidency-at-southern-seminary-sbts.

2) Ibid.

3) Aaron Cline Hanbury, "Twenty years and counting:: Mohler reflects on his presidency of Southern Seminary," http://equip.sbts.edu/publications/tow ers/twenty-years-%E2%80%A8and-counting-%E2%80%A8mohler-re flects-on-his-presidency-of-southern-seminary, page 1.

4) *The Washington Times*, "Mohler shakes up Southern Baptists," September 19, 2003, www.washingtontimes.com/news/2003/sep/19/20030919-1056 16-9435r, page 1.

5) Aaron Cline Hanbury, page 1.

6) Ibid.

7) Ibid., page 4.

8) Albert Mohler, "How Will We Live Now? Francis Schaeffer's 'How Should We Then Live' After 40 Years," October 27, 2016, www.albertmohler. com/2016/10/27/will-live-now-francis-schaeffers-live-40-years, page 1.

9) Wikipedia, "Albert Mohler," https://en.wikipedia.org/wiki/Albert_Mohler, page 2.

10) Aaron Cline Hanbury, page 2.

11) Ibid., page 3.

12) Ibid., page 4.

13) Ibid.

14) Wikipedia, "Southern Baptist Theological Seminary," https://en.wikipedia. org/wiki/Southern_Baptist_Theological_Seminary, page 1.

15) Aaron Cline Hanbury, page 5.

16) Ibid.

17) Broward Liston, "Interview: Missionary Work in Iraq," *Time* magazine, April 15, 2003, http://content.time.com/time/world/article/0,8599,443800,

00.html, page 1.

18) Wikipedia, "Albert Mohler," page 2.

19) Albert Mohler, "Strengthen the Things that Remain: Human Dignity, Human Rights, and Human Flourishing in a Dangerous Age — An Address at Brigham Young University," February 25, 2014, www.albertmohler.com/2014/02/25/strengthen-the-things-that-remain-human-dignity-human-rights-and-human-flourishing-in-a-dangerous-age-an-address-at-brigham-young-university/, page 2.

20) Ibid.

21) Ibid.

22) Albert Mohler, "This is How Religious Liberty Dies — The New Rules of the Secular Left," April 7, 2015, www.albertmohler.com/2015/04/07/this-is-how-religious-liberty-dies-the-new-rules-of-the-secular-left, page 1.

23) Ibid., page 2.

24) Ibid., pages 2-3.

25) Albert Mohler, "The Gathering Storm: Religious Liberty in the Wake of the Sexual Revolution," April 3, 2017, www.albertmohler.com/2017/03/21/gathering-storm-religious-liberty-wake-sexual-revolution, page 1.

26) Albert Mohler, "Religious Liberty and the Right to be a Christian," July 19, 2016, www.albertmohler.com/2016/07/19/religious-liberty-right-christian, page 2.

27) Albert Mohler, "America and the Culture of Vulgarity — No End in Sight," December 12, 2013, www.albertmohler.com/2013/12/12/america-and-the-culture-of-vulgarity-no-end-in-sight, page 1.

28) Ibid., page 2.

29) Albert Mohler, "God, the Gospel, and the Gay Challenge — A Response to Matthew Vines," April 22, 2014, www.albertmohler.com/2014/04/22/god-the-gospel-and-the-gay-challenge-a-response-to-matthew-vines, page 1.

30) Ibid., page 2.

31) R. Albert Mohler, Jr., *We Cannot Remain Silent: Speaking truth to a culture redefining sex, marriage, & the very meaning of right & wrong* (Nashville, TN: Nelson Books, 2015), page 41.

32) Ibid., page 110.

33) Ibid., page 117.

34) Ibid.

35) Albert Mohler, "Why Can't Christians Just Join the Revolution?" November 16, 2015, www.albertmohler.com/2015/11/13/why-cant-christians-just-join-the-revolution, page 2.

36) Ibid.

37) Albert Mohler, "A Gavel Falls on Marriage: The Proposition 8 Decision," August 5, 2020, www.albertmohler.com/2010/08/05/the-gavel-falls-on-marriage-the-proposition-8-decision, page 1.

38) Ibid., page 3.

39) Albert Mohler, "'It is Going to Be an Issue' — Supreme Court Argument on Same-Sex Marriage Puts Religious Liberty in the Crosshairs," May 4, 2015, www.albertmohler.com/2015/04/29/it-is-going-to-be-an-issue-supreme-court-argument-on-same-sex-marriage-puts-religious-liberty-in-the-crosshairs, page 2.

40) Ibid.

41) *Southern News*, "Mohler responds to Supreme Court's same-sex marriage decision," June 26, 2015, http://news.sbts.edu/2015/06/26/mohler-responds-supreme-courts-same-sex-marriage-decision, page 3.

42) Ibid.

43) Ibid., pages 3-4.

44) Albert Mohler, "Fifty Shades of Grey: The Evolution of Pornography," February 23, 2015, www.albertmohler.com/tag/fifty-shades-of-grey, page 1.

45) Ibid.

46) Ibid., page 2.

47) Ibid.

48) Ibid, page 3.

49) Albert Mohler, "Coming to a Doctor's Office Near You? The New Abortion Strategy," July 19, 2010, www.albertmohler.com/2010/07/19/coming-to-a-doctors-office-near-you-the-new-abortion-strategy, page 1.

50) Albert Mohler, "'A Lot of People Want Intact Hearts These Days' — Planned Parenthood, Abortion and the Conscience of a Nation," July 15, 2015, www.albertmohler.com/2015/07/15/a-lot-of-people-want-intact-hearts-these-days-planned-parenthood-abortion-and-the-conscience-of-a-nation, page 2.

51) Ibid., page 3.

52) Ibid.

53) Albert Mohler, "Must We Believe in the Virgin Birth?" December 15, 2011, www.christianity.com/bible/must-we-believe-the-virgin-birth-11643205.html, page 1.

54) Ibid., page 2.

55) Ibid.

56) R. Albert Mohler, Jr., *We Cannot Remain Silent*, page 183.

Chapter 11: Franklin Graham

1) William Martin, *A Prophet With Honor* (New York: William Morrow & Co., 1991).

2) Michael D'Antonio, "Playing it Safe in the Pulpit" (a review of *A Prophet With Honor*),http:// articles.latimes.com/199-11-10/books/bk-2227_1_billy-graham-s-success.

3) Tim Graham, "Newsweek Slams 'Theological Bully' Franklin Graham, Tilting His Politics 'Hard to the Right,'" http://newsbusters.org/blogs/tim-graham/2011/05/17/newsweek-slams-theological-bully-franklin-graham-tilting-his-politics-ha#sthash.ixG2YCNl.dpuf.

4) John Westen, "Billy Graham's Son Franklin: Gay lifestyle is 'a sin' and 'I want to warn people,'" www.lifesitenews.com/news/billy-grahams-son-franklin-homosexuality-is-a-sin-and-i-want-to-warn-people, page 2.

5) Derek Penwell, "Franklin Graham is Still the Worst Thing to Happen to God in a While," *The Huffington Post,* 03/05/2015, www.huffingtonpost.com/derek-penwell/franklin-graham-obama_b_6809080.html.

6) Ibid., page 2.

7) Michael W. Chapman, "Rev. Graham: Secularists Are 'Anti-Christ' and 'They've Taken Control of Washington," *CNSNews,* January 30, 2015, http://cnsnews.com/blog/michael-w-chapman/rev-graham-secularists-are-anti-christ-and-they-ve-taken-control-washington.

8) Ibid.

9) Franklin Graham, "Franklin Graham Points to Jezebel Scriptures to Describe America," *CharismaNews,* 02/12/2015, www.charismanews.com/opinion/48265-franklin-graham-points-to-jezebel-scriptures-to-describe-america.

10) Ibid.

11) GLAAD, "Franklin Graham," www.glaad.org/cap/franklin-graham.

12) Franklin Graham, "Franklin Graham Points to Jezebel Scriptures . . ." page 2.

13) Ibid.

14) Franklin Graham, "Hollywood: Entertaining Ourselves to Death," *AFA Journal*, September 2014, page 17.

15) Ibid.

16) Ibid., page 16.

17) Ibid.

18) Ibid.

19) Ibid.

20) Franklin Graham, "Cowards or Overcomers: Standing Strong," *Decision* magazine, July/August 2014, pages 4-6.

21) Ibid., page 4.

22) Ibid.

23) Ibid., page 6.

24) Ibid.

25) Katherine Weber. "Franklin Graham: There is 'No Compromise' on Abortion, Gay Marriage," *The Christian Post*, 05/18/2012, www.christianpost. com/news/franklin-graham-there-is-no-compromise-on-abortion-gay-mar riage-75146.

26) Franklin Graham, "Only One Solution to End Violence," Billy Graham Evangelistic Association, 02/04/2013, http://billygraham.org/story/only-one-solution-to-end-violence.

27) Brian Montopoli, "Does America Hate Islam?" *CBS News*, 08/19/2010, www.cbsnews.com/news/does-america-hate-islam.

28) Jennifer Leclaire, "Urgent Call for Intercession Over Franklin Graham," *CharismaNews*, www. charismanews.com/opinion/watchman-on-the-wall/ 48410-urgent-call-for-intercession-over-franklin-graham.

29) Carrie Dedrick, "Franklin Graham: Muslims Who Kill Christians Are Emulating Muhammed," *ChristianHeadlines*, 03/13/2015, www.charisma news.com/opinion/watchman-on-the-wall/48410-urgent-call-for-interces sion-over-franklin-graham.

30) Cathy Lynn Grossman, "Franklin Graham wants Obama to step in on Prayer Day slight," *USA Today*, 05/04/2010, http://usatoday30.usatoday.com/news/ religion/2010-05-05-graham05_st_n.htm.

31) Michael W. Chapman, "Graham: 'True Followers of Jesus . . . Cannot Endorse Same-Sex Marriage,'" *CNSNews*, 05/16/2014, http://usatoday30. usatoday.com/news/religion/2010-05-05-graham05_ST_N.htm, page 1.

32) Ibid., page 3.

33) Billy Graham Evangelistic Association, "Franklin Graham Speaks Bluntly About Transgender Bathrooms," *CharismaNews*, 02/20/2015, www.charis manews.com/opinion/48402-franklin-graham-speaks-bluntly-about-trans gender-bathrooms.

34) Kristy Etheridge, "Franklin Graham: 'I'm not going to run,'" Billy Graham Evangelistic Association, 01/28/2015, http://billygraham.org/story/franklin-graham-im-not-going-to-run.

35) Carrie Dedrick, "Franklin Graham Delivers Easter Message with Warning of 'Anti-Christian Bias,'" *ChristianHeadlines*, 04/06/2015, www.christian headlines.com/blog/franklin-graham-delivers-easter-message-with-warning -of-anti-christian-bias.html.

36) Elwood McQuaid, "Is America a Christian Nation?" *Israel My Glory* magazine, March/April 2015, page 6.

37) Bible Prophecy Blog, "Rev. Graham: Christians Need to Get Involved in Politics," 01/31/2015, www.bibleprophecyblog.com/2015/01/rev-graham-christians-need-to-get.html.

38) Michael Gryboski, "Franklin Graham Calls on Pastors to Speak Out on Abortion, Homosexuality; Says 'God Hates Cowards,'" 05/22/2014, www.christianpost.com/news/franklin-graham-calls-on-pastors-to-speak-out-on-abortion-homosexuality-says-god-hates-cowards- 120265.

39) Andra Varin, "Franklin Graham: Obama Has 'Shaken His Fist' at God," *Newsmax*, 05/10/2012, www.newsmax.com/Newsfront/franklin-graham-obama-gay/2012/05/10/id/438661.

40) Alexandra Jaffe, "Obama takes fire for Crusades comparison," *CNN*, 02/07/2015, www.cnn.com/2015/02/06/politics/obama-isis-crusades-com parison, page 3.

41) Jessilyn Justice, "Franklin Graham Rebukes Obama," *CharismaNews,* 02/09/2015, www.charismanews.com/us/48219-franklin-graham-rebukes-obama.

42) Billy Graham Evangelistic Association, "Franklin Graham Launching 50-State Decision America Tour in 2016," 04/15/2015, http://billygraham.org/story/franklin-graham-launching-50-city-tour-in-2016.

43) Ibid.

44) Kyle Mantyla, "Franklin Graham To Save America With Right-Wing 'Prayer Rallies' In All 50 States Before 2016 Election," *Right Wing Watch*, 05/12/2015, www.rightwingwatch.org/content/franklin-graham-save-ameri ca-right-wing-prayer-rallies-all-50-states-2016-election.

Chapter 12: Robert Jeffress

1) Michael J. Mooney, "How First Baptist's Robert Jeffress Ordained Himself to Lead America,"*D Magazine*, January 2012, www.dmagazine.com/pub lications/d-magazine/2012/january/the-savior-robert-jeffress-of-first-baptist-dallas, page 17.

2) BookReporter, "Robert Jeffress," www.bookreporter.com/authors/dr-robert -jeffress, page 1.

3) Michael J. Mooney, page 4.

4) The Alan Colmes Show, "Dr. Robert Jeffress: Same-Sex Marriages Are 'Counterfeit,'" https://radio.foxnews.com/2014/07/28/dr-robert-jeffress-same-sex-marriages-are-counterfeit, page 1.

5) Samuel Smith, "Megachurch Pastor Robert Jeffress: Satan 'Delivered' Islam to Muhammad, Following Islam Will 'Lead You to Hell,'" *The Christian Post*, May 12, 2015, www.christianpost.com/news/megachurch-pastor-robert-jeffress-satan-delivered-islam-to-muhammad-following-islam- will-

lead-you-to-hell-139026/#yvfFOrjiIckBW5Jd.99, page 2.

6) Brian Tashman, "Jeffress: Jews, Mormons, Muslims And Gays Are Going To Hell," October 8, 2011, www.rightwingwatch.org/post/jeffress-jews-mormons-muslims-and-gays-are-going-to-hell, page 1.

7) Brian Tashman, "Jeffress Says Satan Is Behind Roman Catholicism," October 8, 2011, www.rightwingwatch.org/post/jeffress-says-satan-is-be hind-roman-catholicism.

8) Brian Tashman, "Jeffress: Jews, Mormons, Muslims And Gays Are Going To Hell," page 1.

9) Michael Gryboski, "Texas Megachurch Pastor Says Obama Will 'Pave Way' for Antichrist," *Christian Post*, November 8, 2012, www.christian post.com/news/texas-megachurch-pastor-says-obama-will-pave-way-for-antichrist-84639, page 1.

10) Charlie Butts, "Pastor: 'Wimpy' won't cut it in culture war," *One News Now*, December 13, 2012, www.onenewsnow.com/church/2012/12/13/pastor-wimpy-won-t-cut-it-in-culture-war, page 1.

11) Michael J. Mooney, page 8.

12) Tammi Reed Ledbetter, "Criswell's leadership, vision, influence cited by Jeffress, Patterson, Hawkins," *Baptist Press*, January 17, 2002, www.bpnews.net/12465/criswells-leadership-vision-influence-cited-by-jeffress-patterson-hawkins, page 1.

13) Michael J. Mooney, page 13.

14) *Pathway to Victory*, "About Dr. Jeffress," https://ptv.org/about-ptv/who-is-dr-jeffress. Page 1.

15) Michael J. Mooney, page 5.

16) Ibid., page 14.

17) Robert Jeffress, *Twilight's Last Gleaming,* (Franklin, TN: Worthy Publishing, 2012).

18) This edited version of Dr. Jeffress' speech was presented at the 2013 Lamb & Lion Annual Bible Conference. It is reproduced here with the consent of Dr. Jeffress.

19) *Time* Magazine, "Read the Sermon Donald Trump Heard Before Becoming President," January 20, 2017, http://time.com/4641208/donald-trump-robert-jeffress-st-john-episcopal-inauguration, page 1.

20) Ibid., page 2.

21) Ibid.

22) Ibid.

23) Ibid., page 3.

Chapter 13: Jonathan Cahn

1) Jonathan Cahn, *The Harbinger* (Lake Mary, FLP: Charisma House, Front Line Books, 2011).

2) Ibid., page 49.

3) Biographical information supplied to the author by Jonathan Cahn in an email message.

4) Ibid.

5) Ibid.

6) Dave Mosher, "Harbinger author Jonathan Cahn: Who is he, what does he believe, and is he heretical?" https://davemosher.wordpress.com.2013/02/05/heretical-harbinger-author-jonathan-cahn-who-is-he-and-what-does-he-really-believe, page 1.

7) Ibid.

8) Wikipedia, "Jonathan Cahn," https://en.wikipedia.org/wiki/Jonathan_Cahn, page 1.

9) Hope of the World Ministries, www.hopeoftheworld.org.

10) Cahn, *The Harbinger*, page 20.

11) Ibid., pages 20-21.

12) Ibid., page 21.

13) Ibid., pages 21-22.

14) Ibid., page 22.

15) Ibid., page 54.

16) Ibid., pages 191-215.

17) Ibid., page 206.

18) Ibid., page 208.

19) Ibid., page 201.

20) Ibid., page 213.

21) Jonathan Cahn, "The Following is the Transcript of the Key Note Address Jonathan Gave at the Presidential Inaugural Prayer Breakfast — Message," January 21, 2013, www.facebook.com/notes/jonathan-cahn-official-site/the-following-is-the-transcript-of-the-key-note-address-jonathan-gave-at-the-pre/558000007557020.

22) Ibid., pages 2-3.

23) Ibid., page 7.

24) Jonathan Cahn, "Jonathan Cahn's Address at the Presidential Inaugural Prayer Breakfast, January 20, 2017, Washington, D.C.," www.charisma

news.com/opinion/watchman-on-the-wall/62623-jonathan-cahn-s-last-words-to-obama-and-charge-to-president-trump, page 1.

25) Ibid., page 2.

26) Ibid.

27) Ibid., page 3.

28) Ibid.

29) Ibid.

30) Ibid., page 4.

31) Ibid., page 9.

32) Ibid.

33) Ibid.

34) Grant Phillips, "My Two Cents on the Harbinger," www.raptureready.us/featured/phillips134.html, page 1.

Chapter 14: Is America Doomed?

1) David R. Reagan, *Living for Christ in the End Times: Coping with Anarchy and Apostasy*, (McKinney, TX: Lamb & Lion Ministries, 1st edition in 2000 and 2nd edition in 2016).

2) Albert Mohler, "Character in Leadership — Does it Still Matter?" June 24, 2016, www.albertmohler.com/2016/06/24/character-leadership-still-matter.

3) Politico Staff, "Full text: Donald Trump 2016 RNC draft speech transcript," www.politico.com/story/2016/07/full-transcript-donald-trump-nomina tion-acceptance-speech-at-rnc-225974, page 8.

4) Bob Eschliman, "Decision America Tour Event Draws Only This Many People," www.charismanews.com/politics/events/54244-decision-america -tour-event-draws-only-this-many-people, page 1.

5) David R. Reagan, *A Prophetic Manifesto* (McKinney, TX: Lamb & Lion Ministries, 2012), pages 9 and 33.

6) Bob Russell, "Message for a Rebellious Nation," sermon delivered at the Lamb & Lion annual Bible conference in July 2015.